The Book of
Faerie Spells

CHERALYN DARCEY

ROCKPOOL

For dearest and loveliest Ella Risebrow, a true Faerie.
I am blessed with your generous inspiration and friendship.

Those who don't believe in magic will never find it.
Roald Dahl

A Rockpool book
PO Box 252
Summer Hill
NSW 2130
Australia
rockpoolpublishing.com
www.facebook.com/RockpoolPublishing

ISBN 978-1-925682-87-8
A catalogue record for this book is available from the National Library of Australia.

First published in 2019
Copyright Text © Cheralyn Darcey 2019
Copyright Design © Rockpool Publishing 2019

Cover design by Richard Crookes
Internal design by Jessica Le, Rockpool Publishing
Typesetting by Typeskill
Printed and bound in China

10 9 8 7 6 5

The information presented in this book is intended for general inquiry, research and informational purposes only and should not be considered as a substitute or replacement for any trained medical advice, diagnosis, or treatment. All preparations and information about the usage of botanicals presented in this book are examples for educational purposes only. Always consult a registered herbalist before taking or using any preparations suggested in this book. No responsibility will be accepted for the application of the information in this book.

Contents

Welcome, Blossom

I am delighted to share with you this treasury of spells that I have crafted with the energy and magick of the worlds of the Faerie. I have travelled the paths of particular Faeries and their stories from all over the world, across many cultures and throughout time to bring their wisdom to you. Among them are also spells I have woven for you that embody aspects of those Faeries known as Nymphs, Brownies, Elves and Pixies, and of Sidhe and Leprechauns.

Although this book is mainly about Faeries of myth and legend, you will recognise others I have included from more modern literature. Their inclusion is important: I believe that those who describe the Faeries of their imagination and hearts in books, plays and music are moved by the energy that the Fae impart to this world.

Before we start, you must promise me that you will take my advice and follow closely all I share with you about the Fae in this book of spells, for the Faerie folk do not like to be upset, meddled with or taken advantage of. Many, indeed, are not all that pleasant to humans as their lives and business have nothing to do with us so, out of respect and for your safety, I have not included them in this book.

All Faeries are guardians of the natural world and have a special place in their hearts for flowers. In this book you will find a scattering of spells that focus on a flower and the Faerie of that flower. These are my special Faerie spells and I hope they help you discover for yourself the Faeries that I know are tending silently the blossoms in your own garden, as well as woodlands, fields and parks.

Read well the section 'Working with Faerie' and please ensure that you follow the opening and closing of each spell carefully because even the most benevolent and helpful of the Faerie folk will not tolerate rudeness or excuse ignorance in those who wish to work magically with them.

Please take the time to explore more about each of the Faeries I have shared with you. I have included some important resources that will help you understand their world and work more respectfully with them.

Enjoy this book of Faerie spells! I wish that it brings you much happiness and wonderment and fills your heart with Faerie goodness.

May Nature bless you always, but I hope that you too will be the blessing that Nature needs!

Bunches of blessings,

Cheralyn

Ḣow to Use Ḃhis Book

It's never an easy task to create a book of magick instruction to suit everyone. We are all on different paths, with different beliefs and varying levels of experience and I do not believe that these things should bar anyone from experiencing or practising Nature Magick. In order to be safe and work safely for others and your environment, you must first educate yourself in these ways of working. Make sure you read through all the sections of this introduction as they will give you this knowledge. It is simple but vital when creating and casting spells.

Those more experienced in spellcrafting and casting, or who have dedicated and defined paths in their own beliefs, may be able to skim the following instruction pages and dive straight into the spells, experimenting and exploring new paths which may open up, enhance or complement their work. However I suggest that everyone read through the first section in order to familiarise themselves with the foundations on which I have presented this book of Nature Magick.

Whether you are a complete beginner or have some experience, Section One will provide a good grounding in safe and best practice when creating and casting spells. This section also explains, in detail, what a spell is and how it works.

I have shared sixty spells that I have written over my life. They focus on Faeries and their energies with an emphasis on plants and their flowers, and are arranged in smaller chapters by their use so that you can quickly find a spell that suits your needs. Make sure you observe the instructions I have given and any instructions you already use each time you are creating and casting spells.

All steps to using each spell are clearly explained along with simple, everyday ingredients and tools to create them. I also share additional interesting and helpful tips with each spell to enrich your experience working with Nature, so you can get to know the Faeries a little better.

At the end of this collection, I provide a special journal – a place to keep your own spells. In preparation for creating your own spells, I have included a simple guide to writing your own magick and then a collection of beautiful pages that you may use to keep your Faerie spells together with mine.

What if you don't have access to your own plants?

As wonderful as it would be to access every plant on earth, no matter where you found yourself, the reality is that you cannot. I have given you alternate plants that you may be able to source and that hold similar energies, but I would also encourage you to dry your own plants when they are available and create or source essences, candles, incenses and other botanical treasures from trusted suppliers, so you always have a magickal apothecary to rely on.

What if you don't have access to a private outdoor space?

Some of the spells in this book suggest that you cast them outdoors, however you may not have access to your own garden or have a private nature reserve nearby. It is understandable that you may not feel comfortable creating a magickal spell in public or be able to hold the focus required with an audience. In this case, I suggest you create an indoor sacred space. Plants, flowers, an open window and images of Nature can all help create an area that will help you connect with Nature for your spell casting.

What if you don't have plants at all?

To further focus energy or to connect with plants when you do not have access to them, imagery in the form of artwork, photos, your sketches or oracle cards can be used. I feel it is very important to see the plant to connect with its unique energy.

SECTION ONE

What Is a Spell and How Does It Work?

What Is a Spell and How Does It Work?

A spell is a combination of ingredients, tools, actions and focus, which come together energetically to create change. Timings (when you cast your spell) can also be observed to ensure added power.

✿ TIMINGS

Timings can be moon or astrological phases, seasonal times and also correspondences that connect with days of the week or hours of the day or night.

I have included simple, broad timings in the spells in this book. These include Moon Phase, Day of the Week and Time of the Day. Observing these will give your spell work a boost because working in line with the time of Nature is working in synchronicity with what is going on around you and provides stronger focus for your intentions. Please note, however, that the timings I suggest for each spell in this book should be seen as a guide only: sometimes a spell is needed immediately and you are far better not to wait.

For more information about timings and their significance, see page 152.

❦ INGREDIENTS

The ingredients you gather together to create a spell will all have correspondences to your intention. In a way, they illustrate what it is that you want to happen. They will support the things you wish to happen because they have similar meanings and energies. These meanings and energies may also assist you in removing something. Correspondences also help us find substitute ingredients for our spells when what is prescribed is not available, and I will give you suggestions with each spell. For more information about correspondences, see page 151.

❦ TOOLS

Tools are additional items that you can use to help create your spell. Here are just a few examples of tools used in spellcrafting and casting:

» cloths to set your spell up on (*usually in colours which align with the energy of the spell*)
» wands and staffs to direct and enhance energies
» divination tools such as tarot and oracle cards, crystal balls, pendulums and runes to provide clarity
» drums, bells (*musical instruments and music express your intentions*)
» practical items such as a double boiler or alternative (*for example, a saucepan with a heat-proof bowl inside*), glasses, cups, vases, lidded jars or bottles, bowls and cutting tools.

The way you put a spell together, the words you may recite, the things you actually do to cast your spell are the actions that bring it all together. These focus your intention, put you squarely in the path of the outcome and strengthen the relationship between the energies of the ingredients and the tools you are using. This all combines to raise energy in order for magick to happen.

❧ WHY WOULDN'T A SPELL WORK?

Not many things in life work all the time. External factors influence them; maybe they are not put together properly; sometimes it is just not meant to be. I'm sitting here writing my book for you on my laptop. I love my little Apple, but it's rather clunky at times and has its moments. It closes down for no apparent reason, loses files, can't be bothered accepting my Airdrops and decides I need to look at all the files with a certain keyword except the one I want! It appears to have a mind of its own. My computer is working but not always the way I expect because outside influences are affecting it, which is one reason your spells may not work exactly as you expect either.

You cannot change another person's free will and this is also why spells do not work at times. Perhaps the consequence of the spell will adversely affect another or counter their stronger will, which you might not even be aware of. Another reason a spell may not work is because other energies have greater strength at that moment or they may in fact be leading you to a better eventual outcome.

Spells work when the person creating and casting them fully believes in what they are doing and has a strong, focused intention with a good connection to the energies of their spell and the outcome. While perhaps changing things for personal benefit, the outcome is still generally in keeping with a good outcome for all involved without forcibly changing anyone's free will.

❧ HOW TO CREATE AND CAST A SPELL

When you are using the spells in this book, please ensure you do so safely – and that's not just keeping burning candles well attended. Working with energies to create magick requires you to take responsibility for what you are doing, for yourself and the world you live in. There are many ways you can do

this and there are also ways of life and beliefs with their own rituals which ensure safety and power in spellcasting.

Most safety measures include a way to protect yourself and those around you. A way to mark the beginning of the spell or opening the space is usually next. There will be words, meditation, music, chants or actions which will help you focus on the task at hand, and then there will be a way to release the energy, perhaps to give thanks and to close the space.

This is a simple and safe way to cast a spell, but you must also read the following section on working with Faeries to ensure you are working with care and honour with these Nature beings.

Protect and Open

Before you can begin, it's important to establish protection from negative energies. There are various ways you can achieve this but whatever way you use, make sure you always protect yourself and your space. You may wish to use a smudging method, by burning Sage or other plants, or spraying with a smudging mist. You can also visualise or draw a circle around you and your spell with your finger in the air, then fill your circle with white light. If you are aligned with certain deities, elementals or guides, you may wish to ask for their assistance in providing protections. A very simple and effective protection method is to light a white candle while visualising the light cleansing, clearing and protecting.

Focus Intention

Sit or stand still for a long moment and imagine your outcome. Really see it in your mind and complete your picture with exact times, places and events. At this time, before you cast your spell, you may like to write your intention down and say it out loud to get yourself fully focused and your energy aligned with what it is you are about to create.

Cast Spell

In each of the farie spells I have shared with you, I have set out very specific steps to create your spell and explained why I've used them. In the final section, I've provided instruction on creating your own spells. Casting your spell is simply what you do to make the spell happen. While casting your spell, you must maintain your focus on your intention.

Release, Close and Ground

Once you have completed your spell, you will need to release the power you have raised in creating it. Releasing the spell will be explained in each spell I share with you, but you can also do this by simply saying 'I release the power I have raised' or 'It is done' or by putting out your white candle if lit.

Grounding is the way you bring yourself back from your spellcasting time. Clapping your hands, ringing a bell or placing your bare feet or hands on the earth are all ways to ground yourself.

❧ CONNECTING WITH FAERIES FOR MAGICKAL WORK

Because Faeries are guardians of our botanical world and this book has a strong emphasis on plants and their flowers, when working with the spells in this book, you will be connecting with real Nature Magick through the energies of Faeries. You will be walking in their world, doing things their way and sometimes entering their secret places and sharing their special magick. But there are many different types of Faerie found throughout the lands and not all of them are as friendly as you might think.

I want you to be safe, physically and spiritually, so here are a few tips for working with Faeries while creating magickal spells:

Take only what you need and never damage plants
You should do this anyway, but Faeries take a particularly dim view of those who over-harvest, cause damage or are wasteful. Always leave a small offering in place of what you have taken. A dash of milk, a small piece of bread, a lovely piece of ephemeral art created from what you can find in Nature (for example stones or fallen petals).

Leave tokens and offerings
We all like to be acknowledged, but you should never thank the Faeries verbally: they may feel you are making light of their work. Instead, leave them offerings of milk, ale, honey, cake or bread and butter. They love these treats.

How to avoid being taken by Faeries

Show Faeries respect, be polite, leave them offerings and never ever accept any gifts from them. Once a Faerie gives you a gift that you accept, they are allowed to ask you to do anything or for you to give them anything. When you are creating spells, you are asking them, politely, to work alongside you, not for you.

❧ FAERIE RESOURCES

If you wish to work with Faeries, you should learn all you can about them and I'd like to share with you some of my favourite authors and their valuable Faerie works:

Carding, Emily, *Faerie Craft* (Llewellyn Publications, 2012)

Cavendish, Lucy and Conneeley, Serene, *The Book of Faery Magic* (Blessed Bee Publishing, 2010)

Engracia, Andrés, *Fairy Dust Inspiration Cards* (Rockpool Publishing, 2017)

Turgeon, Carolyn, Nuth, Grace and the editors of *Faerie Magazine*, *The Faerie Handbook* (Harper Design, 2017)

❧ INGREDIENTS AND TOOLS FOR SPELLS

Tools and magickal ingredients can be obtained from bricks-and-mortar stores and online, but always be guided by your feelings when making purchases. Make sure you feel comfortable and positive about these businesses because their energies will transfer. Anything that comes into your space to use for spell work has no doubt passed through various other hands and should be magickly cleansed. Do this by placing the items under running water, smudging with smoke or placing them underground in suitable wrapping or a container for a night.

Create a Faerie Garden

Many plants and their flowers are used in this book so although often you can buy them or find them growing in Nature, perhaps you would like to grow your own dedicated Faerie garden.

All plants come under the guardianship of Faeries but there a few that are treasured Faerie favourites and no magickal garden should be without them. These will encourage the Fae to live in your garden and also provide you with a very good foundation to stock your apothecary. (Please independently check on the toxicity of each plant and its suitability for your garden, family and pets as you should avoid those considered noxious weeds in your area.

Be sure to plant a bed of Thyme (*Thymus vulgaris*) just for the Faeries. This should be well tended and never harvested, as they will love building their homes right there. Plant a separate Thyme bed for your own use.

» Basil (*Ocimum basilicum*)
» Bluebell (*Hyacinthoides* spp.)
» Chamomile (*Matricaria chamomilla*)
» Clover (*Trifolium* spp.)
» Cowslip (*Primula veris*)
» English Daisy (*Bellis perennis*)
» Fairy Fan Flower (*Scaevola aemula*)
» Fairy Iris (*Dietes grandiflora*)
» Foxglove (*Digitalis purpurea*)
» Hollyhock (*Alcea* spp.)
» Honeysuckle (*Lonicera* spp.)
» Jasmine (*Jasminum officinale*)
» Lavender (*Lavandula* spp.)
» Marigold (*Tagetes* spp.)

- » Mint (*Mentha* spp.)
- » Nettle (*Urtica dioica*)
- » Pansy (*Viola* spp.)
- » Primrose (*Primula vulgaris*)
- » Ragwort (*Jacobaea vulgaris* syn. *Senecio jacobaea*)
- » Rose (*Rosa* spp.)
- » Rosemary (*Rosmarinus officinalis*)
- » Sage (*Salvia officinalis*)
- » St John's Wort (*Hypericum perforatum*)
- » Strawberry (*Fragaria* spp.)
- » Thyme (*Thymus vulgaris*)
- » Verbena (*Verbena* spp.)

SECTION TWO

A Collection of Faerie Spells

FAERIE GARDEN
AND NATURE
SPELLS

Celandine Faerie Guide Flower Spell

This spell helps you find a Flower Guide either for a specific purpose, time or event. This could even be your Flower Guardian for life. Chelidonium majus, commonly known as Greater Celandine or just Celandine, is the perfect flower to assist you in finding a Flower Guide as it sharpens insight and offers clear vision. The Celandine Faerie will open communication with the flower world and provide you with greater understanding of your dreams and any messages you may receive.

Timings
New Moon, Monday, Late Night

Find and Gather
» Celandine (*Chelidonium majus*) flowers
» 3 lengths of dried but still flexible vine, each about 30–60 cm (*12–24"*) long
» florist wire or string
» a length of green ribbon
» a notebook and pen

The Spell

Sit outside on the ground, preferably in a garden or place of wildflowers.

Take the vine lengths and plait together while saying:

One is me, one is you, one is land,

Together entwine and together we band.

Wrap the ends in florist wire and then bend and secure together to form a circle.

Tuck the Celandine flowers in around your vine circle.

Attach the ribbon and hang the wreath above your bed.

Leave your notebook and pen handy beside your bed. You might dream of your flower during the night and if you do, be sure to write it down or draw it straight away. If you do not dream of it, go for a walk and observe the flowers you come across. You will definitely be drawn to your Flower Guide through appearance, scent or even artwork.

Once you find your Flower Guide, take your vine circle and bury it under a large tree, thanking the Celandine Faeries for their help.

Wearing a fresh Celandine flower when appearing as a defendant in a court of law will ensure that you receive a positive result in your favour from a jury and judge.

Celandine blossoms when migrating swallows arrive in summer and they leave when it finishes flowering. This gives rise to another common name for this plant: Swallowwart.

Curupira Animal Protection Spell

Wearing green and with flame-red hair, the Curupira are Faeries from Brazil who look after animals with a passion, especially to protect them from hunters. This spell requires a bit of craft work, but it is very easy and helps focus your energy completely on the animal/s you wish to protect. You might like to create this spell for a particular animal you know or for a whole species.

Timings
Waning/Dark Moon, Tuesday, Midday/Dusk

Find and Gather

» a green candle
» a brown candle
» a picture of the animal you want to protect (*size: a little smaller than A4*)
» a sheet of A3 cardboard
» scissors
» a selection of old magazines
» a glue stick
» a pencil
» matches

The Spell

Light your green candle and say:

Lord and Lady of the Wild Wood,

Faeries of the Animals,

I call you all to help me,

Protect and provide.

Hold up the picture of the animal/s to the sky for a moment.

Light the brown candle and say:

Healing help for animals far and wide.

Cut out your animal picture and place on the A3 sheet of cardboard. Use the old magazines to cut out colours, objects and words that you feel will provide healing, strengthening energy and fill the shape of the animal by gluing them down with the glue stick. Once complete, place it before the candles and leave it until they burn down.

Please use recycled materials for the very best energy to help your animals. When you feel the energy has done all it can, recycle the poster you have made or upcycle it into a frameable, hanging piece of art for your home.

Curupira are fascinating beings who live in the forest and are known to create illusions. Along with their flame-red hair and green outfits, these male-like Faeries have feet that are turned backwards to confuse hunters that may be trying to track them. They often make a very high-pitched whistling sound.

Foxglove Faerie Magick Garden Spell

Foxgloves hold the energy of appreciation and patience, and they assist with the breaking of habits. Faeries that work with Foxgloves are also very focused on working with energy for good. These are all really positive and useful facets you need to help grow magick – good safe magick – in your garden. You will need a tree in your garden to create this spell but if you do not have one, create something resembling a tree from natural objects. Perhaps driftwood piled together or a fallen branch, or create the form of a tree with sticks bound with string and staked in the ground.

When handling Foxglove, be extra-careful: although a healer, it is poisonous and can affect your heart. Wear gloves and wash your hands after handling it, and never reuse any tools used in this spell for food purposes.

Timings
Waxing Moon, Monday, Morning

Find and Gather
» a Foxglove flower (*Digitalis purpurea*) that you haven't picked from your garden (*see box*)
» rainwater collected in your garden
» a clear glass bowl
» a glass misting bottle
» a white Rose (*Rosa* spp.)

The Spell

Foxglove, although a healer, is a poisonous plant and great care should be taken when using. We will be creating a flower essence to ensure it is as safe as possible to use without diluting the power of this majestic flower. Essences created from flowers and plant matter capture the energy of the plant and any trace of the botanical will be miniscule, however care should still be taken.

Place your bowl in the sunlight in your garden and fill with rainwater.

Gently dip the Foxglove flower into the water and say:

Faerie caps, foxes' gloves,

Energy flow for a garden of love.

Gloves of Fae, Faerie caps,

Take your magick and around my garden wrap.

Let the Foxglove go and then gently release the petals of your Rose one by one and place in a circle around your bowl. While doing this, picture in your mind a garden that is thriving under your care and that is filled with magick and love. Leave this for exactly an hour. When you return, decant the water into the glass spray bottle and label your Foxglove Faerie Flower Essence. Go to your selected tree and bury the Foxglove and Rose petals under the tree, giving thanks.

Spray a heart-shaped pattern on your tree with the flower essence you have made every day at the same time (if you can) until the bottle is empty.

Never pick your own foxgloves! If you have some in your garden, then for this spell prop your bowl up under the flowers and gently bend them into the water. Picking foxgloves that you have grown or letting them become unkempt will make any Faerie very cross with you.

Planting Foxgloves in the garden is generally regarded as inviting the Faeries to live there, but Foxgloves are also associated with negativity: in some areas, it is thought that bad Faeries gave foxes the flowers to wear on their paws so they could hunt unheard.

Faerie Nature Glitter Boundary Spell

Magickal sprinkles are a handy item to make ahead to use when needed.
They spread the energy to a space or place quickly and can be carried very
easily. You do not need to use a lot; just a tiny pinch will be enough.

Timings
Waning Moon, Saturday, Dusk

Find and Gather

- » 2 tablespoons of dried Lavender heads (*Lavandula* spp.)
- » 1 tablespoon of dried Pine needles (*Pinus* spp.)
- » 1 tablespoon of dried Rosemary (*Rosmarinus officinalis*)
- » 2 tablespoons of Sage (*Salvia officinalis*)
- » 1 tablespoon of powdered Sandalwood (*Santalum album*)
- » 4 tablespoons of colourful dried flowers of your choice
- » 4 tablespoons of cornflour (*cornstarch*)
- » 1 tablespoon of black Pepper (*Piper nigrum*), ground
- » a mortar and pestle or spice grinder
- » a large mixing bowl

» a wooden spoon

» a lovely glass storage jar with lid

» a small pouch or container to carry

The Spell

Grind each herb individually, add it to the mixing bowl then
say the following:

Lavender calm,

Cleanse and protect.

Pine give us courage,

Longevity be.

Rosemary hold,

The memory keep.

Sage share your wisdom,

And peace for all time.

Chop the colourful dried flowers, fold into the herbs with
the cornflour and say:

Soft white light,

Faerie Goodness impart,

Let none cross the line,

With dark in their heart.

Store in the glass jar for up to 6 months in a cool
dark place.

To use: carry in pouch or smaller container and sprinkle on
ground to cast magickal circles or to add a magickal protective
or cleansing border to homes, gardens and other places.

Sprinkling powders
are left in situ if
you want to add an
energy to a place but
swept away if you
want to rid a place of
certain energies. The
Sprinkles absorb them
for you first.

Don't be tempted
to add actual glitter
to this spell as it is
not friendly to the
environment. The
colour and brightness
that the Faeries love
is provided through
the use of real Nature
glitter – the flowers!

Meadowsweet Faerie Pendulum Spell

Creating a pendulum from flowers and other natural treasures is a way to connect with the garden and Faeries to help shine a little illumination on your path ahead. Using a tea-leaf infuser is a very quick way to create this pendulum but you could also create it from a small square of cloth suspended from a length of ribbon or even make your own if you are handy at jewellery-making.

Timings
Dark Moon, Wednesday, Midnight/
Night

Find and Gather

» a teaspoon of meadowsweet
   flowers (*Filipendula ulmaria*)
» a tea-leaf infuser, the kind that
   looks like a ball on a chain
» 1 tiny moonstone
» a square black cloth
» 4 moonstones of any size
» a gold coin
» a clear quartz crystal point with
   a flat bottom
» a small black mojo bag to keep the Faerie pendulum in

The Spell

Your meadowsweet flowers can be either fresh or dried. Place them in the tea-leaf infuser along with the tiny moonstone. Take it outside and hang in a tree overnight. Before you leave it, say:

> *Yes and no,*
> *No and yes.*
> *No longer the answers,*
> *Will I have to guess.*

To use: You can use your Faerie Pendulum at any time but each time you will need to 'tune' it. To do this, spread out the black cloth and place the gold coin in the centre with the clear quartz on top and a moonstone in each corner of the cloth. Hold the Faerie pendulum over the clear quartz and ask a question to which you know the answer is 'Yes'. Make a note of how the pendulum reacts: perhaps it goes to a certain crystal, stays still or rotates a certain way. This action will be the 'Yes' answer for future questions. Then ask a question to which you know the answer is 'No' and a third to which you know the answer is 'Perhaps'. Note each action, ready for your divination session.

Once you are ready, ask your questions, making sure they can be answered 'Yes', 'No' or 'Perhaps'.

At the end of the session, store your Faerie pendulum in the black bag. Always cleanse the crystals and the gold coin under running water or by passing through Sage smoke.

Try making a pendulum with a Rose suspended from a string or ribbon. This is a very popular natural divination tool that is especially good for questions surrounding love, romance and relationships.

According to traditional folklore in the United Kingdom, if you inhale the scent of fresh meadowsweet flowers you can gain the gift of second sight, enabling you to converse with Faeries.

Tylwyth Teg Faeries Bumper Harvest Spell

*From Wales in the United Kingdom come stories of the Tylwyth Teg.
These are flower- and garden-loving Faeries that are described as being
incredibly beautiful and just under a metre in height (3 feet). They reside
in a secret land known as Annwn or sometimes the 'Otherworld'. This
place can only be reached via entrances hidden in bodies of water.*

*Use this spell when planting a new garden bed or crop. It will ensure
added protection for your plants
and more vigorous growth. You
will have more luck encouraging
the Tylwyth Teg if you have a
water feature in your garden.*

Timings
Full Moon, Sunday, Daytime

Find and Gather
- » 1 cup of milk
- » ¼ cup of honey
- » a large pot or cauldron
- » a wooden spoon
- » 4 large wooden garden stakes
- » 4 moss agate crystals

The Spell

Before you plant out your garden bed or crop, set up all your gathered ingredients and tools where you will be gardening.

Into your pot or cauldron, pour the milk and say:

Tylwyth Teg, your help I ask,

To garden well and come harvest bask,

In gratitude with you.

Take the honey and drizzle into the milk and say:

Sweet nectar I offer you,

Milk to sustain,

Will you watch over my plants,

Leaf and the grain?

Stir with the wooden spoon, making the shapes of the harvest you are planting. If you are planting tomatoes, trace the shapes of actual tomatoes. If you are planting sunflower seeds, then trace the shapes of sunflowers. Visualise the harvest you seek and see it healthy, strong and beautiful and say:

Tylwyth Teg together we will share,

All that we grow with love and with care.

Dip the end of each large wooden garden stake in the milk and honey and then stake it firmly in the ground at each corner of your garden bed. Place a green moss agate crystal next to each on the side closest to the garden bed. Sprinkle the rest of the milk and honey around the perimeter of the bed.

The Tylwyth Teg are generally friendly and helpful to humans and the females sometimes even marry human males. However they are very enamoured of blond male human children and have been known to steal them. In some parts of Wales, it was customary to dress very young boys in girls' clothing to protect them.

Moss agate is known as the 'gardener's crystal' or stone. It will not only increase your own gardening skills if worn, the crystal will also improve the growth of any plant if placed in the soil beside it.

Dryad Nature Protection Spell

The Dryads are a type of Ancient Greek Faerie, a nymph of the forest. Each is aligned with their own tree. So for this spell, find a tree you are drawn to in the area you wish to offer protection to. If you are not in that area, find an example of a tree you know grows in the area or even botanical material from such a tree, such as essential oils, essences, bark, flowers, leaves or twigs.

Timings

Waxing Moon, Saturday, Midday

Find and Gather

» a tree
» matches
» a green candle
» a cup of spring water
» a pinch of salt
» a small green square of fabric
  8 × 8 cm (*3.2 × 3.2"*)
» 30 cm (*12"*) green ribbon or
  string
» a coin
» a stone

The Spell

If you cannot be with an actual tree, create the form of a tree with sticks, bound with string and staked in the ground. This can be very simple but will assist in raising the energy you need for this spell. Use the botanical material described in this spell's introduction to anoint or add to the tree form.

Light your candle and say:

Light the way for positive change.

Add the salt to the water and stir with your finger. Draw a circle around the tree and say:

Dryad good, true and fair,
Please help me raise additional care.

Place the coin and the stone on the fabric square and draw it up into a pouch. Tie the ribbon around it and tie to the tree and say:

Abundance in blessings,
And Nature protection,
Together let us make
This important connection.

This spell must be undertaken very carefully and respectfully, so you do not anger the Dryad. Have some cake and honey handy and if by some chance you feel you have raised some objection, leave the offering and go!

The Dryads are a type of Nymph, the caretakers and the spirits of the trees. Each has a different name, such as the Hamadryades – nymphs of poplar and ash trees; the Oreiades – nymphs of conifers; and the Daphnaie – nymphs of laurel trees.

Thyme Faerie See the Fae Spell

You will end up with a deep moisturising eye balm and a spell to see Faeries all in one with this Rose-infused botanical blend. The Thyme Faeries hold and will impart, if you ask very nicely, the ability to see all of the Fae world. Using this eye balm regularly will lift the veil for you while giving your eye area a lovely nourishing treatment. For oily and normal skin, dot around the eye area and tap in each evening. For dry and more mature skins, use morning and night. Thyme will also give you courage, strength and lift your spirits if you are feeling unmotivated.

Timings

New Moon, Wednesday, Late Night

Find and Gather

- » 6 tablespoons of shea butter
- » 1 teaspoon of vitamin E oil
- » 3 drops of Rose (*Rosa* spp.) essential oil
- » 1 tablespoon of sweet almond oil
- » 3 sprigs of fresh Thyme (*Thymus vulgaris*)
- » a double boiler or alternative
- » a wooden spoon
- » a small wooden stirrer
- » sterilised jar/s and lid/s

The Spell

Melt the shea butter slowly in the double boiler while continually stirring with the wooden spoon. Remove from the heat and stir in vitamin E, Rose essential oil and sweet almond oil.

Heat the jar/s, fill and take out into the garden.

Place your eye balm somewhere lovely and sit with it.

Taking the Thyme, gently pluck the leaves and drop into the eye balm, saying:

Strengthen my eyes,

Clear my vision.

Open my heart,

To all that's around me.

Stir the Thyme into the balm with the wooden stirrer and say:

I know you are there,

And I'm grateful for your care.

Thyme Faeries,

I thank you.

Put the lid/s on and leave under a plant in flower or a place you feel is particularly magickal in your garden or in Nature for about an hour. Store in the fridge and use within three months.

Ever since people first created gardens it's been a tradition to grow a patch of Thyme just for the Faeries to live in. This was never used but designated as a home for the Fae Folk.

A wash created from Thyme, Marigold and Rosewater will also help you see Faeries. All ingredients must be collected while facing east and left to steep for three days in the sun before using.

Deva Faerie Connection Spell

In Sanskrit their name means 'shining one' which is the perfect way to describe these Faeries, who appear as tiny to small light spheres. Occurring throughout the world, their stories originated in Persia. They live in Nature and are found particularly with flowers in forests and around bodies of water. Devas help us communicate with plants both for our benefit and for that of the plants and the natural world. This spell is excellent for those wishing to work more closely with plants and their flowers.

Timings
Full Moon, Monday, Morning

Find and Gather

» a lovely glass jar and lid
» spring water
» 5 glass marbles
» 2 tablespoons of vodka or rubbing alcohol
» 30 cm (*12"*) of green ribbon
» a green candle
» 2 tablespoons of Pansy petals (*Viola* spp.)
» matches
» a plant you feel a strong connection with, preferably in flower

The Spell

This spell works best if you can perform it next to the plant you feel a connection with, out in Nature where it is growing.

Sit by your plant and set out all the spell ingredients. Sit for a while just listening and watching, then stand and say:

Devas of Nature,

Before you I stand,

To learn and to listen

To all of your plans.

Place the marbles in the jar and pour in the vodka/rubbing alcohol, then sprinkle in the Pansy petals and say:

My love of Nature,

I promise is true,

Thank you Devas,

I honour you.

Top up with the spring water. Seal and tie the green ribbon around the neck of the jar. Leave in places where you would like a stronger connection with the land and the plants that grow there. You will need to empty and remake each month.

If you want to create flower essences and especially if you are studying the vibrational qualities and meaning of plants and their flowers, this spell is an excellent way to ensure you open the channels of communication.

Pansies are entwined with love in all its forms but importantly for this spell, they deepen the bonds of love and strengthen relationships.

Trädandar Faerie Wishes Tree Spell

The Trädandar are Northern European spirits of the trees who communicate through the rustling of leaves. Taking the form of very tiny Faeries, they can also shapeshift into women and owls. A special tree on your property can be dedicated as a wishing tree. Many cultures feature stories of trees that can grant your heart's desire, usually by tying a piece of cloth or ribbon to a branch. In the United Kingdom (particularly in Cornwall) and Ireland these trees are known by many names including May Bushes, Rag Trees, Faerie Trees and Clootie Trees.

Timings
Full Moon, Sunday, Night

Find and Gather

» Select a tree that you would like to become your Faerie Wishes Tree
» 120 cm (47") of silver ribbon
» 120 cm (47") of gold ribbon
» 120 cm (47") of white ribbon
» a small white bag with drawstrings
» 1 tablespoon of Mugwort (*Artemisia vulgaris*) leaves
» an amethyst crystal

The Spell

You might need longer or shorter ribbons, depending on the width of the tree trunk.

Sit on the ground with your back against the tree. Take some time to just sit and listen to the tree and get to know it. You might like to talk to the tree about your plans and see if your tree wants to become a Faerie Wish Tree. If it doesn't, then please find another tree.

When you feel ready, take the three ribbons and tie them all together at one end. Then plait them together while saying three times:

Over and under,

Weaving with wonder,

For you my dear tree,

The ribbons of three.

When complete, tie the ends together. Stand up and tie the ribbons around the tree trunk.

Put the Mugwort in the small white bag with the amethyst crystal and then tie to the ribbon plait. Now say:

Oh Faeries of trees,

Come please listen to me,

This blessed tree shall be,

A place that wishes are set free.

Whenever you have a wish, tie a piece of cloth or ribbon to a branch and make your wish. When the cloth or ribbon fades or falls, your wish will be granted.

Clootie trees are usually found near wells or streams. It is also believed that if you wash an afflicted area of your body with a piece of cloth and then tie it to a Clootie Tree, you will be cured.

Mugwort is traditionally used in divination work and is also a herb that offers protection. You can also use bunches of Mugwort to rid a place of negative spirits as they do in Japan.

FAERIE LOVE
AND FRIENDSHIP
SPELLS

Rose Faerie New Love Spell

All Faeries have a great regard for Roses. They cannot help but want to protect and care for them and this great affection spills out of the flowers themselves in the form of love. This spell involves a bit of good old-fashioned syrup-making. The Rose Faerie love potion that results is a lovely addition to drinks, on fruits and desserts and drizzled on cakes. Or anywhere you would like to infuse a little extra love. To find a new love, sip a tiny amount first thing every morning.

Timings
Full Moon, Friday, Morning

Find and Gather

- » 1 cup of organic edible red Rose petals (*Rosa* spp.)
- » 1 cup of rainwater
- » a teaspoon of lemon juice
- » 1 cup of sugar
- » 2 tablespoons of pectin
- » a wooden spoon
- » a heat-proof glass/Pyrex or non-reactive saucepan
- » sterilised jars or bottles with lids

The Spell

Tear the Rose petals by hand as small as you can into the saucepan. Pour the rainwater over them, place on heat and bring to the boil.

Once boiling, turn off heat source and leave the saucepan, covered, for 30 minutes to steep.

Before you leave, say:

Rose Faeries of love and of heart,
New love I seek to make a new start.
Please bring your magick,
To find the right one.
I'll be ever so grateful,
Once this spell we have done.

After 30 minutes, strain the Rose petals and reserve them, then return the water to the original saucepan. Add the sugar and return to the heat. Bring to the boil. Be careful not to let it boil over. Stir to dissolve the sugar while saying three times:

Sweetness of love.
Around and be found.

Add the lemon juice and keep stirring while saying:

A tang of passion,
Sharp but delightful.

Once the sugar is completely dissolved, add the pectin and keep boiling for a minute.

Remove from heat. Heat the jar/s or bottle/s and fill.

Take the Rose petals and bury under a tree in the garden/park, giving thanks to the Rose Faeries for their assistance.

Faerie secrets, 'sub rosa' – our modern-day plaster ceiling roses come to us via the Ancient Roman practice of hanging a single Rose from the ceiling above a meeting to signify that anything said 'under the Rose' was a secret. Perhaps you might entice the Rose Faeries to whisper a love secret to you this way!

Roses are protected by Faeries, so to encourage them into your garden, plant as many roses as you can. The Fae are sure to want to settle in.

Faerie Heal a Broken Heart Spell

This healing oil balm is wonderful for your skin and can help with scars both inside and out. Calendula is known for its physical healing properties, but it also brings the warmth and power of the sun so can help you step into a brighter tomorrow. Rosehip oil imparts the loving gifts of Roses to help fill your heart with love again as well as rejuvenate your skin.

Timings

Full Moon, Friday, Morning

Find and Gather

» ½ cup of dried Calendula petals (*Calendula officinalis*)
» 2 tablespoons of Rosehip oil
» ½ cup of coconut oil
» 2 capsules of vitamin E oil
» A mortar and pestle or spice grinder
» a saucepan with lid
» a fine sieve
» a sterilised glass jar with lid
» a wooden spoon

The Spell

Grind the Calendula petals well, and while grinding say over and over:

Flowers of the sun,
Bring happiness round.

You might even like to make a little song out of the words.

Once the petals are ground very fine, place in the saucepan with the Rosehip oil and coconut oil over a low heat, stirring until the coconut oil has completely melted. Turn off the heat, put the lid on and say:

Warm my heart,
Warm my life,
A brighter tomorrow,
And no more love strife.

After a few minutes, strain into a warm jar, add the vitamin E oil and stir.

Store in a cool, dry place and cool before use.

To use: Rub a dab on your heart area each morning and say:

Come together and heal,
The pieces that have fallen,
I see a new day,
And new hope I hear calling.

You can also use this powerful healing oil on other areas of your skin that need physical healing — but do not use on broken skin.

This lovely balm can also be used as a hair-repair oil. Rub a tablespoon of it between your hands to warm and then tousle through your hair. Comb through. For very dry hair, you may find you can leave it in. Other hair types, use pre shampoo, leave in for an hour and then wash out.

If you place a Calendula flower under your pillow on Halloween, you should dream of the true man of your dreams.

Ambrosia Faerie Romantic Spark Grow Spell

Ambrosia is a Nymph in Greek mythology and also the food and drink of the Gods. Connecting with her will help you embrace love and all its possibilities openly. Red Rose petals are included for their energies of passion, courage and love. Orange Blossom is very good at moving relationships closer to more romantic and committed levels, and Love-in-a-Mist encourages others to be more open to love.

Timings
Full Moon, Friday, Evening

Find and Gather
» ¼ cup dried red Rose (*Rosa spp.*) petals

» ¼ cup dried Orange Blossom (*Citrus × sinensis*)

» ¼ cup dried Love-in-a-Mist (*Nigella damascena*)

» a red cloth

» a small wooden box with a lid

» a rose quartz crystal

» paper, pens and pencils

» a spoonful of honey

» a small glass of wine

The Spell

Lay the red cloth out on the table, place the wooden box in the centre and put your rose quartz crystal inside. Write down the details of your romantic spark and how you wish it to grow, and place in the box.

Place the dried flowers in the box, eat the spoonful of honey (to sweeten your words and to honour Ambrosia), and say:

Plants of love,

Of passion and of earth,

Live now together,

Under Ambrosia's grace,

And blessings impart.

Add your note, sip the wine and say:

Fanning flame of love you go,

The spark that has started,

Now will grow.

Put the lid on and store the box somewhere central in your home. At times when you want to boost the power of the blessing box, open the box and simply request what you wish to happen. When you do, be sure to thank the box with a little additional sprinkling of any of the flowers.

This blessing box, once created, is opened to release Faerie magick to boost a romantic spark so that it may find the energy to grow. While you cannot change the will of another to make them fall in love, you can make the energy more favourable.

During the Renaissance period, Love-in-a-Mist was worn in the hair of brides to signify their virginity. To give to another means 'Kiss me' and 'I am open to your love'. Perfect for weddings or for any love charm or spell!

Crocus Time to Love Again Spell

Crocuses are used in this spell because they assist those who want to love again. They help instill peace of mind, inspire happiness and, importantly, release the pain of the past. The Crocus Faeries bring new light, mirth and an opening to possibilities. Pink Roses are used in this spell because they inspire not only love but also forgiveness and healing.

Timings
Waxing Moon, Friday, Morning

Find and Gather
» a Crocus (*Crocus* spp.)
» 4 pink Roses (*Rosa* spp.)
» an hourglass
» a compass
» 4 pink rose quartz crystals with points
» a tray of sand (*or you can do this spell at the beach*)

The Spell
For this spell, you will be creating a flower and crystal grid around an hourglass. If your hourglass is less than an hour, you will need to flip it until you make up an hour in time.

On a windless day, spread out your sand on the tray or find a level place on the beach.

Place your hourglass on the sand and say:

This is the hour of time and change,

Love has gone but will begin again.

Using the compass, carefully place each of the pink rose quartz crystals around the hourglass at North, South, East and West, with points facing out, and say:

My love goes out, grows strong and true,

Return to me a heart renewed.

Gently release the pink Rose petals from the flower and create a pattern with them between and around the hourglass and crystals. Then hold your Crocus flower up to the sun to fill it with light. Make the action of pouring the light around your crystal and petal grid and say:

Crocus Faerie, may I ask of you,

To share new light – joyful, good and true.

Place the Crocus on top of the hourglass.

When the hour is completed you can dry and keep the flowers in a box or little bag along with crystals. Hang or keep somewhere that catches the morning sun.

Alternate Flowers

Any type of Crocus can be used for this spell. Roses in pinks or whites are best.

An old tradition tells us that if we plant Crocus in the garden, love and affection will come to us. Be warned that dreaming of Crocus indicates there may be danger in love looming.

Mixed with alum, Crocus was used as an incense by the Ancient Egyptians. It was said that the smoke would enable those who had been robbed to see visions of those responsible.

Iolanthe Clear Away Misunderstandings Spell

The story of the Faerie Iolanthe, misunderstandings, silliness, confusion and an ending in which all live happily ever after is the subject of a very funny operetta Iolanthe, *by Gilbert and Sullivan. This spell taps into the energies required to clear away seemingly never-ending misunderstandings with a Rose Salt Bath. Inhale deeply while you distance yourself from the mayhem in a steamy bath of blossoms. Clear your head and look forward to some balance.*

Timings

Full Moon, Wednesday, Midday/Late Night

Find and Gather

» a bunch of fresh Thyme (*Thymus vulgaris*)

» 1 cup of dried Rose petals (*Rosa* spp.)

» 2 cups of Himalayan salt

» string

» 8 drops of Rose essential oil

» 2 white candles

» relaxing but upbeat music

The Spell

Tie your fresh Thyme bunch to your bath tap with the string, making sure that the running tap water will go over the leaves.

Draw your bath to your preferred temperature and as it is running add the Himalayan salt and Rose essential oil and say:

Faeries of Nature,

Of herb, flower and earth.

Unravel these things,

Then my mind clear, rebirth.

Once the bath is full, place the two white candles where you can see them when lying in the bath. Light each and say:

Light of truth, light the way,

Make clear what is muddy,

Take confusion away.

Sprinkle the Rose petals on the water and say:

Let us be respectful,

Remain as friends.

This misunderstanding,

Now bring to an end.

Put on your music and enjoy a really lovely soak. Do not let your mind dwell on any negativity. If it does, focus on the candles and say the last lines again.

Once complete, scoop up the petals and Thyme and bury them in the garden.

Salt has traditionally been used in many faiths and beliefs to clear away negativity, to purify and to release attachment. It also helps ground and balance.

Roses are known to help lower stress levels, and promote soft and subtle skin. They are also an aphrodisiac. In Ayurvedic medicine Roses used to help detox the body.

Aine See the Light of Love Spell

The Irish Faerie Queen Aine (pronounced awy-ya), is deeply connected with the moon, and with the care and healing of the sacrum (at the base of the human spine). This oil blend spell asks for her assistance in seeing your own light and body in a more positive way and as powerful and strong. It will strengthen self-image and provide positive thought patterns so that you may see the light of love within yourself. Jasmine has been chosen for its own threads of connection with the night, sensual evenings, the moon, and of hope, success and abundance in all things.

Timings
Full Moon, Monday, Night

Find and Gather
» 10 drops of Jasmine (*Jasminum officinale*) essential oil
» 40 drops of Ylang-ylang (*Cananga odorata*) essential oil
» 20 drops of May Chang (*Litsea cubeba*) essential oil
» a handful of Jasmine flowers (*fresh or dried*)
» a large shallow bowl
» spring water or rainwater
» a small round mirror
» a very beautiful sterilised crystal/glass bottle with stopper

The Spell

You are creating an essential oil blend to use diluted in water-mist space sprays or on its own as an anointing oil for candles and magickal tools and objects, as well as in diffusers and burners. This blend can also be added to a carrier oil, such as sweet almond oil for use in massage.

On a full moon night, set the bowl outside on the earth in a place where the bowl will catch the moon's reflection once filled with water. Place the mirror in the bowl then fill the bowl with water, saying:

Faerie Queen Aine,

I see your brightness,

I ask that I see mine too.

Cast the Jasmine flowers upon the water and say:

Purify, cleanse and take away,

The thoughts I no longer need.

Add the essential oils to your bottle then seal with the stopper. Hold over the bowl of water and, swirling the bottle to blend the oils, say:

Within and without,

I am beautiful,

Within and without,

There is no longer doubt.

Pour the water onto the ground and say:

All that no longer does me service, gone.

Litsea cubeba is also known as May Chang and Mountain Pepper. It smells a little like Lemongrass, though slightly warmer in tone. A highly rejuvenating oil, it is known to lift mood and instill energising joy. Magickly, this oil can be used in spells and rituals that celebrate renewal and beginnings.

You can add Jasmine to any love spell to boost its power. This flower has powerful abundance-attracting energies as well as opening pathways to spiritual, self-love and romantic love.

Honeysuckle Faerie Send Happiness Spell

An uplifting, happiness-inducing bath salt blend that is perfect to give to a friend who is feeling down or just as a lovely embrace of your friendship. Honeysuckle Faerie will sprinkle the air with happiness, sweeten dispositions, express devotion and promise unity.

Timings
Full Moon, Monday, Evening

Find and Gather
» 1 cup of Himalayan salt
» ¼ cup of bicarbonate of soda
» 1 teaspoon of dried Honeysuckle flowers (*Lonicera* spp.)
» 1 teaspoon of dried Rose petals (*Rosa* spp.)
» 1 teaspoon of freeze-dried strawberries (*Fragaria* spp.)
» 1 teaspoon of finely grated fresh orange peel (*Citrus* × *sinensis*)
» 5 drops of Bergamot (*Citrus bergamia*) essential oil
» 5 drops of Lavender (*Lavandula* spp.) essential oil

- » 5 drops of orange essential oil
- » a glass mixing bowl
- » a wooden spoon
- » a gorgeous sterilised glass jar
- » a pretty card
- » ribbon (*long enough to make an attractive bow on the neck of your jar*)

The Spell

Mix together the Himalayan salt and the bicarbonate of soda in the glass bowl and say:

Ground and release, earth and peace.

Next, add the Honeysuckle flowers and say:

Happiness come, Happiness stay.

Then add the Rose petals and say:

Love, love, love.

And now the strawberries and orange peel, and say:

Sweeten the brew.

Add the essential oils and mix well. Decant into the gorgeous jar. Write upon the card 'Happiness Bath' and tie it to the neck of the jar with your ribbon.

To use, empty the entire jar into your bath and say:

Faeries of flowers,

Faeries divine,

A bath of blissful sweetness,

Happiness be mine!

Enjoy your blissful bath!

You are not only gifting happiness but also luck with this lovely bath salt gift. To find or give Honeysuckle is considered very lucky. Crushing the flowers on your forehead is said to increase psychic powers.

Find some gorgeous bottles with stoppers to turn the bath salts into truly magickal gifts complete with the spell chant on the lovely card threaded on a ribbon around the neck of the bottle. This spell makes about just over a cup of magickal bath salts.

Folletti Faerie Harmony and Happiness Spell

*The Folletti are an Italian race of Faerie folk who are rarely seen as they
reside in another dimension but they do on occasion shapeshift from their
usual near-invisibility to assume the form of butterflies. They have a very
uplifting and happy Nature and are very friendly if you are lucky enough
to see them. This spell creates a simple tincture that can help lift your
mood. St John's Wort is not suitable for everyone and can be contradictive
with other drugs so check with your doctor first.*

Timings
Full Moon, Wednesday, Midday

Find and Gather
» 2 cups of finely chopped fresh
  Lemon Balm (*Melissa officinalis*)
» 8 teaspoons of dried St John's
  Wort (*Hypericum perforatum*)
» 1 cup of vodka
» A mortar and pestle or spice
  grinder
» a fine strainer
» a large sterilised glass jar with
  lid
» a smaller storage jar

The Spell

Place the Lemon Balm in the jar and say:

> *Negative thoughts be gone,*
>
> *Melissa sweet,*
>
> *Replace with thoughts strong.*

Grind the St John's Wort finely, add to the jar and say:

> *Calming sacred one,*
>
> *Help me be strong.*
>
> *Lift me,*
>
> *Hold me,*
>
> *And I will follow on.*

Pour in the vodka and seal with the lid. Shake well.

Keep in a cool, dark, dry place for two weeks but ensure that you visit it each morning and shake. Each time say:

> *Wake up, wake up,*
>
> *Be happy and bright.*
>
> *Folletti Faeries,*
>
> *Dance in the light.*

After two weeks, strain and bury herb matter, with a few words of gratitude to the Folletti, in a sunny spot in the garden. Decant liquid into small jar.

To use: take a teaspoon each morning in a little juice.

Although the Folletti are a very lovely race of Faerie folk, the males tend to be a little mischievous: it is claimed they love changing the weather suddenly and kicking up the dust to create storms just for fun.

This tincture is created to boost your connection with happiness and to lift your mood but Lemon Balm is also a very powerful love charm herb so don't be surprised if your love life receives a lift, too!

Violet and Pansy Loving Honey Spell

*This loving honey spell will help heal a heart that has been hurt as this is
the specialty of Sweet Violet Faeries. They will also offer protection from
deception, instill loyalty and open to you new options in your love life
going forward. The Faeries who are deeply connected with Pansies inspire
loving thoughts in all those they come in contact with and are very good
at helping you to stay immune to negative thoughts and things that may
harm a relationship.*

Timings
Full Moon, Friday, Morning

Find and Gather
» a handful of organic, clean Sweet
  Violets (*Viola odorata*)
» a handful of organic, clean
  garden Pansies (*V. tricolor* var.
  hortensis)
» organic honey to fill your jar
» a mixing bowl
» a wooden spoon
» a gorgeous sterilised jar with an
  airtight lid

The Spell

Pour the honey into the bowl.

Carefully pick just the petals of your flowers and place in the bowl.

Stir together with the wooden spoon and say with every turn:

Loving thoughts and love-filled hearts.

Once the jar has cooled, bottle your Violet and Pansy Loving Honey.

Store in a cool, dry place.

To use: You can use your loving honey to sweeten teas, in your cooking, by the spoonful and as offerings for Faeries to inspire positive, loving thoughts for you too!

To bring love into a home, drizzle a small heart shape with this honey on the path leading to your front door and say:

Love walk gently, love be kind,
All who step here, in love aligned.

Never pick the first violets of spring; to do so is considered very unlucky. Wait until there is an abundance and then always pick a good bunch, never just a few.

If your love is a sailor then create a Pansy bed in your garden. Bury a handful of sand from the beach in this bed and your love will always think of you and want to return home to you.

Faerie Truffles Happy Gathering Spell

These little joys are perfect to share around when you are at a get-together to ensure happiness. Faeries are known for their love of sweets, treats and milk so these offerings combine all of these, along with a little attracting Faerie sparkle with the addition of pretty sprinkles. Don't forget to leave at least one out for your Faerie friends so they join the festivities too!

Timings
Any Moon Phase, Any Day, Any Time of Day

Find and Gather
» 250 g (*8.8 oz*) of plain sweet biscuits (*cookies*)

» ⅓ cup of cocoa powder

» ¼ cup of desiccated coconut

» ½ cup of finely chopped walnuts

» 395 g (*14 oz*) can condensed milk

» colourful cake-decorating sprinkles

» a large plastic food bag

» a large bowl

» a wooden spoon

» a large flat plate

» a dozen Heartsease flowers (*Viola tricolor*)

The Spell

Place the biscuits (cookies) into a plastic bag and crush finely with a rolling pin. Put into the bowl with the cocoa powder, desiccated coconut and walnuts. Slowly pour in the condensed milk while mixing with the wooden spoon and say:

> *Chocolate so sweet,*
>
> *Tempers be likewise.*
>
> *Milk pure of light,*
>
> *Feed and protect.*
>
> *And walnuts wise,*
>
> *Listen well and advise.*

Place in the fridge for 30 minutes so that the mixture firms. Spread the sprinkles on a plate. Roll tablespoons of the mixture into balls and then roll in the sprinkles. To serve, place a Heartsease flower, or petal, on each truffle.

You can keep these (without the Heartsease flowers) in an airtight container in the fridge for up to four days.

Heartsease flowers are brilliant little merrymakers. They will impart self-forgiving energy, comfort and compassion. Be warned – never pick your Heartsease when they are still damp from the morning dew. To do so is said to bring great misfortune upon your family.

Party like a Faerie and include gorgeous edible flowers, sparkling fairy lights, beautifully scented candles, the prettiest of plates and glassware along with lots of fresh blossoms, plants and herbs. Faeries do love gatherings and they especially like to share sweet cakes, delicious treats and drinks with their friends.

FAERIE HEALING
AND PROTECTION
SPELLS

Alven Faerie Water Energy Spell

These tiny water Faeries are also shapeshifters, liking to change into otters occasionally. They do not have wings, but still fly by riding within bubbles. Generally kind beings, Alven hail from the Netherlands and live in ponds and other waterways. This spell will create a water you can sip through the day to boost your energy. The addition of elderflower will boost your strength, vigour and fortitude, and offer protection. Evening Primrose is added to honour the Alven and for its balancing properties.

Timings
Any/Full Moon, Tuesday, Dusk

Find and Gather
» a beautiful sterilised glass bottle
» spring water to fill your bottle
» An Evening Primrose (*Oenothera biennis*) oil capsule
» a sprig of Elderflowers (*Sambucus nigra*) or a small dash of Elderflower cordial

The Spell

Take your spell ingredients outdoors near a water feature
(such as a pond or fountain) or waterway – choose a location
where you can safely leave your bottle out overnight. Place
the Elderflower sprig or cordial into the bottle and say:

Flower of magick,

Of energy and joy,

Lift up this day.

Fill with the spring water and say:

Faeries of water,

Faeries of flowers,

Please take this water,

And so empower.

Add a drop of Evening Primrose oil and say:

For you, dear sweet Alven,

A flower of night.

Pour a little of the water onto the ground.

Seal and leave your water bottle near the water feature or
waterway overnight.

Sip as you please during the day. Must be consumed
within 24 hours.

If you would like to
invite the Alven to
your garden, you will
need a water feature
and their favourite
night-blooming
flowers. Be very
careful to tend to the
flowers well because
if you do not, they
will seek revenge for
their flower friends.

Everywhere that Elder
grows, it is considered
magickal in some way.
The Druids regard the
tree as the beginning
and the end and
this is because Elder
flowers at the very
beginning of Summer
and the fruit ripens at
its end.

Mallow Faerie True Voice Spell

A sugar scrub infused with the magick of Mallow Flowers which will help us find our true self and speak with our true voice. This lip scrub can be used regularly to give you lovely soft lips and to connect with the magick of the Faeries that look after the Mallow Flowers. You will also find it of great benefit if you have found yourself not speaking the way you know is right. Clear away the negative energy with this lip scrub right away! The beauty of Mallow is that it brings us grace as well.

Timings
Full Moon, Thursday,
Midday

Find and Gather

» 3 fresh Mallow Flowers
  (*Malva sylvestris*)
» 1 teaspoon of sugar
» 1 teaspoon of lemon
  juice
» 1 teaspoon of coconut
  oil
» a mixing bowl
» a wooden spoon
» a small sterilised jar and lid

The Spell

Chop the Mallow Flower petals very finely and place in the mixing bowl.

Add the sugar, lemon juice and coconut oil and mix slowly, saying:

Lip clean and fresh,

Words will now rest.

Mallow Faerie help find,

The voice that is mine.

Once mixed, place in the jar and keep in the fridge and your lip scrub will last about two weeks.

To use: Each time you use the mixture, place a little on your finger and say:

Scrub away,

Words negative gone.

Fresh clear lips,

Share words true and strong.

Rub gently on lips in a circular motion then wipe off.

Mallow Flowers can help return a lost love to you. Place a bunch on your windowsill to prompt them to think of you and the possibility of returning to you.

You can protect yourself from any Faerie magick that is doing you harm. Wear a single Mallow Flower and it will stop negative energy directed towards you. Mallow will also break spells and hexes if worn.

Morgan Le Fey Daily Health Spell

There are many versions of the legend of the half-Faerie, half-human
Morgan Le Fey. Although some depict her in a negative light, she is widely
regarded as a powerful healer. From the magickal Avalon, she was King
Arthur's half-sister and became apprenticed to the great Merlin. Bring
daily health and healing to you by starting with a warming and sharp
drink to boost your metabolism and awaken your mind, spirit and body.

Timings
All Moon Phases, Daily, Morning

Find and Gather

» juice of one lemon (*Citrus ×
  limon*)
» ¼ to ½ teaspoon sized piece of
  fresh Ginger (*Zingiber officinale*),
  peeled and grated
» ground black pepper
» ground cayenne pepper
» ground turmeric
» spring water
» a hand juicer
» a grater
» a lovely drinking glass

The Spell

Pour the lemon juice into the drinking glass and say:

> *Morgan Le Fey, I honour your power,*
>
> *Your goodness and light,*
>
> *With the boost of the sour.*

Add the grated Ginger to the glass to your taste, and say:

> *Warmth and passion,*
>
> *Enfold and inspire.*
>
> *The health and the healing,*
>
> *Alive with a fire.*

Sprinkle in the ground black pepper, ground cayenne and ground turmeric to your taste.

Fill the glass with spring water then drink, making sure to leave a little in the bottom of the glass.

Take this out to the garden and pour it onto the earth, saying:

> *I thank you Morgan Le Fey for your help,*
>
> *Our brew of health, together we drink.*

Adding a few drops of lemon juice to a bowl of water makes a very good negative energy cleanser of magickal tools. The same goes for lemon juice in a bath or shower wash for you.

To mend a friendship or create a new one, place a slice of lemon under their chair when visiting your home. You can also use dried lemon blossoms and fruit in sachets as love charms.

Nephelae Emotion Calming Spell

The Nephelae are Nymphs who look after the clouds and the rain. They take the water from earth up to the heavens. This spell aligns with the correspondences of water which assist with emotions. Use when emotions have been out of control in your home, office, space or when you or those around you are finding it hard to find tranquility and peace.

Timings
Full Moon, Monday, Dusk

Find and Gather

» a few stems of Sweetgrass (*Hierochloe odorata*)
» a large grey scarf, sheet or tablecloth
» rainwater
» a large, flat bowl
» a candle holder (*waterproof*)
» a light-blue candle
» matches

The Spell

Lay your grey cloth out in the area that is a focus of or has experienced emotional turmoil. Place the bowl on top and set your candle holder with candle in the centre of the bowl.

Pour the rainwater into the bowl and say:

Nephelae, Faerie of water and sky,

Can you see from the clouds,

The challenges from up high?

Snap small pieces of Sweetgrass and float in the water and say:

A little gift of sweetness and peace.

Light the candle and say:

Light of tranquility,

Of calm and of peace.

Settle emotions,

The turmoil to cease.

This is a great opportunity to sit and meditate with your spell for a calmer and more balanced environment around you. Once you are finished, pour the water onto the earth and thank the Nephelae.

Sweetgrass is associated with spirituality, healing and peace and is very sacred to the Native Americans who use it extensively in their ceremonies. Braids are woven from the stalks and these are then used in offerings. It is also burned as a smudging herb.

It is strongly suggested that you collect rainwater for this spell to be most successful and that captured during a full moon will be the most powerful when it comes to harnessing the power over emotions. Adding a tablespoon of glycerin to a large sterilised bottle of such water, kept in the fridge, will help the water to last about six months.

Rosemary Faerie Mental Clarity Spell

*Create this solid herbal perfume to carry with you in either a locket
(with a Faerie inscribed on it for extra power) or in a small tin and rub
on your pulse points throughout the day when you need a mental boost
or are trying to find clarity in a situation. You can also simply inhale
the perfume when needed. Rosemary is one of Nature's great memory
enhancers as well as boosting mental strength and helping ensure accuracy
and clarity. Lemon essential oil is included as it will help clear space,
banish negative thoughts and help you find the truth.*

Timings
Full Moon, Wednesday, Late
Night

Find and Gather

» 2 tablespoons of beeswax
  pastilles
» 3 tablespoons of coconut oil
» 10 drops of Rosemary
  (*Rosmarinus officinalis*)
  essential oil
» 5 drops of lemon (*Citrus ×
  limon*) essential oil
» a double boiler or alternative
» a glass jug

» sterilised lockets or tiny tins (*with lids*)

» a spoon

The Spell

Place the beeswax in the double boiler, stir over medium heat
to melt and say:

Gift from the bees,

Hold my spell tight.

A balm of clarity,

Strength and great sight.

Add the coconut oil and stir until melted and well
combined. Remove from heat and pour into the glass jug. Add
the Rosemary essential oil and lemon essential oil and stir
while saying:

Together these oils,

Together they carry,

The spell I will make,

With the blessings of Faerie.

Pour into lockets/tiny tins. Leave somewhere cool and
out of the sun, away from heat so they can set. You can use
other essential oils for this perfume balm but check for skin
suitability and always allergy-test yourself before using.

Rosemary is a herb
that will attract
Faeries when burned.
You can create a
smudge style stick
with long sprigs of
fresh Rosemary that
is bound tightly with
organic string and
hung to dry out.

In some parts of the
world it is believed
that fairies have a
great dislike of lemon
as it is poisonous to
them, so you may
wish to leave the
lemon oil out of this
perfume balm. Then
again, if you feel you
are being mentally
manipulated by
any negative Faerie
energies, leaving it
in may be perfect
for you!

De Grossman Stop Bad Behaviour Spell

*While I do not suggest that you call on these German Black Forest Faeries
to punish anyone who has displayed negative behaviour and worked
against you, tapping into the energies surrounding boundary-making that
the De Grossman live by will help you. The birch tree is found in the Black
Forest, from where the De Grossman hail, and its inclusion in this spell
will bring you protection, build courage and help banish fear.*

Timings
Waning Moon, Saturday, Midday

Find and Gather

» a stick of Birch (*Betula* spp.)

» salt

» a small black tourmaline crystal

» a piece of paper

» a pen with black ink

» matches

» a cauldron or heat-proof bowl

The Spell
Find a quiet place outdoors,
preferably a forest or a place with
trees and not at your home or place
of work. With your Birch stick,

draw a circle in the earth, large enough for you to sit within.
Sprinkle salt along the line and say:

> *Line of protection,*
> *Line of light,*
> *With Birch to hold you,*
> *All will be right.*

Write the wrongdoing on the piece of paper and say:

> *Here the wrong be held,*
> *Within this circle,*
> *Shall be felled.*

Place the cauldron or heat-proof bowl in the centre of the
circle and then burn the paper in it while saying:

> *De Grossman would change this,*
> *Take it into the night,*
> *Within the great forest,*
> *And then make it right.*

Place the black tourmaline crystal in the cauldron or bowl
and shake while saying:

> *I stop this behaviour,*
> *It is gone with the night*
> *Tomorrow we shall see,*
> *All will be right.*

Bury the ash and the crystal and rub away your circle.

The De Grossman were said to drag naughty children into the Black Forest and torment them until their behaviour improved.

Birch has been used throughout time in exorcism. It was thought that being hit with a Birch branch would drive demons from the body and this is probably how the cane used in corporal punishment came to be.

The Vila Faerie Battle Spell

In Russia, there is a powerful race of Faeries that are not only protectors of the wildlife and forests but also of people who are fighting causes that they agree are true and just. They are also known to dispense justice to human men who wrong women and to provide healing to those injured in battles they agree with. In this spell, the wind is used to raise up energy, call the Vila to you and empower your personal energy so you are strong enough to carry on in any challenges that involve conflict.

Timings
Full Moon, Tuesday, Morning/Midday

Find and Gather
» a tree
» a piece of music featuring a female singer
» 4 ribbons, one each of blue, red, yellow and green, 15 cm (6") long
» 4 Nasturtium flowers (*Tropaeolum majus*)
» a cupcake or muffin

The Spell

The song you select should be very empowering and make you feel energised, confident and strong. The wind directions and colours stated here are traditional Northern Hemisphere correspondences. You may wish to reverse them in the Southern Hemisphere.

On a day when the wind is stirring, find a tree with branches you can reach.

Start playing your selected music and, tying the blue ribbon to a branch, say:

West Wind, action I bid you bring.

Then tie on the red ribbon and say:

South Wind life and energy raise.

Next, tie on the yellow ribbon and say:

East Wind, balance and soothe as you will.

Lastly, tie on the green ribbon and say:

Powerful Wind of North the outcome I seek.

Then state what you would like your outcome to be.

Place the Nasturtiums at the base of the trunk of the tree.

To complete this spell you must thank the Vila and to do so, say:

Powerful and true my battle be,
I thank you all for fighting beside me.
Now take these ribbons as you will,
A sweet meal too in honour and goodwill.

Lay the cupcake or muffin at the base of the tree and leave overnight.

The inclusion of Nasturtium flowers in this spell will help you achieve victory because that is the energy they impart. They also help restore harmony, especially in places where conflict has occurred, and planted in your garden will deter unwanted visitors.

Thought to have been women who lived unfulfilled and frivolous lives, the Vila are now stuck between this world and the next. They are very beautiful in appearance, have divine singing voices and are also fierce warriors with power over the wind.

Hibiscus Faerie Purification Spell

There is nothing as soothing as a beautiful cup of tea and this brew combines the power of purifying herbs and ingredients to help you not only recover from any negative experience but also cleanse the unwanted energy away. The Hibiscus Faerie will impart happiness while recharging and renewing your focus and feelings. Honey is included as a natural healer and Ginger will give you a little uplifting zest while relieving tension. Lemon will clear and clean away any remaining toxicity.

Timings
Waning Moon, Saturday, Midnight/
Midday

Find and Gather

- » 1 heaped tablespoon of Hibiscus tea-leaves (*Hibiscus* spp.)
- » 1 tablespoon of grated fresh Ginger (*Zingiber officinale*)
- » boiling water
- » a beautiful teapot
- » a white tablecloth
- » a white candle
- » matches
- » tongs

- » paper and pen
- » a heat-proof bowl
- » a teacup and saucer
- » A fresh Sage leaf (*Salvia officinalis*) for each cup or a small pinch of dried Sage leaves
- » lemon wedges (*Citrus × limon*) and honey to serve

The Spell

Set a table with the white cloth and light your candle. Place the Hibiscus tea-leaves and grated Ginger in the teapot and fill with the boiling water. Set it on the table and say:

Flower from the places of sun,

Flower lift energy for all and for one.

Ginger release.

With the pen and paper, write down the situation or thing you need purified and burn it in the candle flame while holding with tongs. Then, dropping it into your heat-proof bowl, say:

In the flame be gone.

Pour your tea into the teacup, add a squeeze of lemon and sweeten with a little honey. Stir with a Sage leaf and add to cup if you like. Sip your tea and visualise your situation or thing becoming gradually clearer and lighter until finally it's gone.

Hibiscus flowers are floated on water to use in scrying in the Pacific nation of Dobu. Patterns that the flowers create can be interpreted, as can the directions they may take. Moving towards you would be seen as an affirmation, while moving away would be a negative answer.

Known for their love- and passion-inducing properties, these gorgeous flowers can also be used in love spells.

Trooping Faerie Change Luck Spell

*The Trooping Faeries are considered the aristocracy of the Sidhe Faeries,
a noble race of Faeries descended from the Tuatha dé Danann, who are
still thought to live in Ireland today. Trooping Faeries are travellers who
gained their name for the long and beautiful processions they create while
moving throughout the land. Wearing splendid clothing, they play various
instruments and have a love of celebration, singing and dancing. Trooping
Faeries bring good fortune and happiness. With a tendency for stealing
pretty glittery treasures and of playing pranks on humans, this spell is
formed to respectfully appeal to their nature while inviting better luck into
your home.*

Timings

Any Moon Phase, Friday, Sunset

Find and Gather

» a white Carnation (*Dianthus caryophyllus*)

» a yellow Rose (*Rosa* spp.)

» your favourite upbeat piece of music

» a drum or any portable musical instrument you can play

» a collection of shiny treasures such as jewellery, coins or crystals

» a piece of cake

» honey

» a beautiful bowl or dish

» a gorgeous plate

The Spell

Do this spell for six days in a row, beginning on a Friday.
Each sunset, stand in your front doorway, facing outwards,
set your flowers next to your door and play your music.
Play along on your instrument. A makeshift drum or other
instrument is also completely acceptable.

When finished say:

The Trooping Folk of the Sidhe,

Here in my home to you I bid.

Good luck please bring into my home,

Bring with you from the places you roam.

Once you have finished, place the bowl in your kitchen
and fill it with the shiny treasures. Place the plate with the
cake on it, drizzled with a bit of honey, next to the bowl and
say:

Welcome Troop,

Relax and please rest.

I'm grateful for your presence,

And the good luck you bring, blessed.

The next morning, bury any cake that's been left in the
garden and be sure to change the shiny treasures each day a
little to add variety for the Troop.

Yellow Roses indicate
that you are open
to friendship: they
say 'welcome' and
'please return'. White
Carnations are very
helpful in bringing
good luck.

Trooping Faeries
hold trees incredibly
sacred, especially
Oaks and Hawthorns.
If you can bury the
remaining cake under
one of these, then do
so. To damage one
of these trees in any
way will anger greatly
the Trooping Faeries
and bring their wrath
upon you.

Queen Mab's Secret Keeper Spell

Shakespeare's play, Romeo and Juliet, is the first appearance in English literature of Queen Mab, the Queen of the Faeries, who is considered to also be Titania and Medb of Welsh folklore. Thought to be beautiful, possessing a wildness about her and having power over the oceans and the stars, she is also the keeper of all the secrets of the world. This is classic 'spell box' magick, which involves raising energy to empower a box to be forever magickal. In this case, you will be making a place to keep secrets safe.

Timings

New Moon, Saturday, Late Night

Find and Gather

- » rock salt
- » white Rose petals (*Rosa* spp.)
- » a clear quartz crystal
- » a beautiful black box
- » a small handkerchief-sized black cloth
- » a black candle
- » a candle holder
- » matches
- » a pen with black ink
- » paper

- » a pair of flame-proof tongs
- » a heat-proof bowl
- » a length of black ribbon, about 30 cm (*12"*)

The Spell

Create a circle from the rock salt and then sprinkle with the white Rose petals and say:

> *Queen of the Faeries, Queen of secrets true,*
>
> *Within this circle I shall safely share with you.*

Place the black candle in its holder in the centre, light it and say:

> *The light shall fall upon what is in my heart,*
>
> *Then fall to be safe in the quiet of the dark.*

Sit before the candle and write down your secret/s on the paper.

> Place the clear quartz on the paper and say:
>
> *Witness my words and hold on to this light,*
>
> *Queen Mab, a crystal for you,*
>
> *For your work on this night.*

Holding the paper with the tongs, burn in the candle flame and drop into the heat-proof bowl to capture the ashes. Once cool, put the ashes onto the black cloth, fold and place in the box. Tie the black ribbon around the box and, while holding it up to the sky, say three times:

> *Secret/s stay put, secret/s stay quiet.*

Bury the crystal at the base of a very large tree as thanks to Queen Mab.

A Scottish tradition says that if you see a white Rose blooming in Autumn (*Fall*), then there will be a wedding very soon.

The Faerie Queen Mab is described throughout literature as being both 'good' and 'bad'. Sometimes evil, uncaring, mean – even dangerous – and at other times generous, kind, beautiful and willing to grant humans their wishes. She is truly a being of light and dark, of shadow and light.

FAERIE HOME
AND FAMILY
SPELLS

Lavender Faerie Sweep Away Spell

If you are experiencing negativity, bad luck or challenging times in your home, work or other space, then sweeping with a physical broom will disrupt and clear these energies. Adding some help from the Faeries of Lavender will provide cleaning magick and leave protection behind with each sweep. Pick Lavender with as long a stem as possible. The found stick will be the broom handle, so size is personal preference.

Timings
Waning Moon, Saturday, Midnight

Find and Gather

» a big bunch of Lavender (*Lavandula* spp.)
» a found stick about 30 cm (*12"*) in length
» a white sheet
» a white candle
» matches
» a roll of waxed linen thread
» a pair of scissors

The Spell
Spread the white sheet over your doorstep or front door area. This is to provide purity and protection to your magickal creating time.

Leave your door open, sit down with your gathered treasures, light your candle and say:

Light and flame,
Purify and protect

Strip about 6 cm (3") of foliage off the end of each Lavender stalk.

Lay a row of Lavender stalks around the end of the broom (bare ends against the stick with flowers forming the end of your broom head) and tie securely with one loop of waxed linen thread. Repeat rows until you have used up all your Lavender. You may wish to slightly overlap rows up and down to create a graduated end to the Lavender.

As you do this, talk to the Lavender Faeries. Let them know how much you appreciate them looking after these flowers and helping them to grow so beautifully, and how grateful you are for their use. Praise the flowers and thank them for their energy and love.

Once you have all the flowers attached to your broom, wrap the waxed linen thread around the stalk ends to neatly bind and tidy up the attachment area. Tie off securely.

While doing the binding, say three times:

Round and round the spell is made,
Round and round with light and flame,
A broom of Fae,
A broom is made.

At the end of the handle, tie a loop of ribbon to hang your broom from. Keep it just inside and to the left of your front door and use it to clear away the doorstep and also throughout the house whenever you want to sweep away negative energies and add protection to your home.

Faerie brooms like this one work a lot better if they have a name and this is because they feel more a part of the household and family, so be sure to name yours.

To help make a wish come true, place a single sprig of Lavender under your pillow before you go to sleep and if you dream of your wish, it is said that it will come true.

Gårdstomte Pet Healing Spell

*Found in Sweden, the Gårdstomte is a rural Faerie being, usually with
the appearance of an elderly man, who has a very strong connection to
animals and the people who live on the land. This bottled oil spell appeals
to these qualities and will help you bring healing energy to any ailing pets.
Thyme raises the positive aspects of the Fae energy, Tea tree will protect
and heal, and using a flower from the area where your pet resides will
alert the Gårdstomte to your aid.*

Timings

Full Moon, Saturday, Midnight

Find and Gather

- » porridge
- » butter
- » a flower from the place where your
  pet lives
- » a sprig of Thyme (*Thymus vulgaris*)
- » 4 drops of Tea tree (*Melaleuca
  alternifolia*) oil
- » sweet almond oil
- » a brown candle
- » a beautiful bottle

The Spell

Like most Fae folk, the Gårdstomte need to be thanked and they have a special fondness for fresh porridge and butter so before you begin this spell, make a small batch and leave it outside your front door and say:

Dear hard-working Gårdstomte,
A meal to give you comfort.
Then I kindly ask for your guiding,
For my pet with love all abiding.

Light the brown candle and then add the flower and the sprig of Thyme to the beautiful bottle. Fill with the sweet almond oil and say:

Flower of land,
Herb of the Fae.
Mix together and see,
A healing well made.

Stand the bottle next to the candle until it burns out.

Go to your pet and draw a circle in the ground or on the floor around it lightly with your finger dipped in the oil and say:

Within is healing.

Repeat as necessary.

A dab on the body of some animals (not birds or fish) may also be used for additional healing.

Although these hard-working Faeries will help you increase your good fortune, never offer the Gårdstomte gifts of clothing as they will consider themselves to have climbed in social status and stop working. You must also never treat animals badly in any way as the wrath of these Faerie beings is unrelenting.

You do not need a garden to find your flower for this spell. Any flower connected in some way to your area will help empower this spell. Go for a walk and find a lovely flower, or even a flowering weed. Make sure it is safe for human and animal use.

Bean Tighe Faerie Family Helper Spell

You can think of the Bean Tighe as a kindly motherly helper, usually invisible, with a great affection for families, especially children. They hail from Ireland and to invite them into your home, an offering of strawberries and cream is best. In this spell, such an offering is created along with a lovely permanent blessing and sign of gratitude for this very generous and helpful Faerie.

Timings
Waxing Moon, Friday, Evening

Find and Gather

» a large bowl of the nicest strawberries (*Fragaria* spp.) you can find
» 1 cup of double (*heavy*) cream
» 2 tablespoon of honey
» a mixing bowl
» a whisk or rotary hand beater
» a very pretty, small bowl with a lovely spoon
» a strawberry-scented candle
» matches
» a candle holder – this is to be dedicated to the Bean Tighe

The Spell

Place the mixing bowl and whisk or beater in the freezer for 30 minutes. Chilling the equipment ensures that your whipped cream will be perfectly light and delicious. Place the strawberry-scented candle in its candle holder near your front door and light it while saying:

Bean Tighe, you are welcome here,

Our family increase,

With your help and your love,

We shall live in happy peace.

In the kitchen, place the cream in the chilled mixing bowl, drizzle in the honey and then whip until stiff peaks form. In the small bowl, arrange a few strawberries and dollop on the cream. Set it outside your front door and say:

You are welcome to join us,

Do come inside,

Our family embraces,

Bean Tighe by our side.

The light here shines for you

And always shall be.

Leave out overnight and clean up the next day. Any leftover is to be buried in your front garden or under a tree near your property. Light the candle whenever you want to send additional gratitude to this Faerie being and be sure to create some strawberries and cream treats every now and then.

You could use an electric mixer for this recipe, but it is far preferable to use a whisk or at the very least, a rotary hand beater. When you are creating food for magickal purposes, the more you can slow the pace and focus your energy, the stronger and more powerful your spell will be.

Faeries like berries because they are sweet, and they are small and easy to manage. If you do not have strawberries available, you could try other delicious berries that are in season.

Faerie Chai Time Sleepy Tea Spell

This calming and delicious tea is boosted with a magickal spell to bring you a good night's sleep. You must make sure you leave out an offering so your dreams are not disturbed by any Faeries who feel like making mischief when the moon rises.

Timings
Any Moon Phase, Any Day, Evening

Find and Gather

- » 1 cup of milk or milk substitute
- » 1 small Cinnamon stick (*Cinnamomum verum*)
- » 1 Cardamom pod (*Elettaria cardamomum*)
- » 1 teaspoon of chopped Valerian root (*Valeriana officinalis*)
- » 2 teaspoons of Rooibos (*Aspalathus linearis*) tea-leaves
- » a few drops of pure Vanilla (*Vanilla planifolia*) extract
- » ¼ teaspoon ground Nutmeg (*Myristica fragrans*)
- » honey to sweeten
- » a mortar and pestle or spice grinder

- » a fine strainer
- » a saucepan
- » a lovely cup and saucer
- » a beautiful tiny saucer

The Spell

This spell makes a cup for one person, so increase amounts as needed to serve more of the family. Perhaps you could make a lovely big pot for everyone before bedtime.

Grind the Cinnamon and Cardamom and say:

Spice of the earth,

Ground and make me quiet,

Grant me sleep,

Through all of the night.

Place the milk, Nutmeg, Rooibos tea and Valerian in a saucepan, add the Cinnamon and Cardamom and bring to a simmer for five minutes, but do not allow to boil.

Remove from heat, strain and pour into your cup.

Add the Vanilla extract and say:

Balance and Peace.

Stir in honey (amount to your taste) and say:

Faerie I honour you,

Light and good natured,

Please bring me sweet dreams,

Under these silver moonbeams.

Place a teaspoonful on the tiny saucer and leave at your front door along with the spices you have strained as an offering for the Faeries.

Rooibos tea is native to South Africa and contains magnesium and calcium which promotes calm and helps induce sleep. The magnesium also decreases the stress hormone cortisol.

Other herbs that the Faerie love and use to help them sleep that you might like to add to your tea are: Thyme (*Thymus vulgaris*), Lavender (*Lavandula* spp.) and Chamomile (*Matricaria chamomilla*).

Faerie Dreams Banish Nightmares Spell

This is a soothing and calming bath bomb to enjoy before you pop into the land of slumber. This mixture makes one bath bomb so if you are in the mood to make more, simply multiply the spell. Lavender is included for its powerful anti-stress properties and Heartsease for calming the heart and nerves and also because it is the perfect Faerie Nature glitter with its pretty confetti-like colours. Flowers are always sure to attract good Faerie dreams!

Timings

Full Moon, Sunday, Dusk

Find and Gather

- » 4 tablespoons of bicarbonate of soda
- » 4 teaspoons of citric acid
- » 1 teaspoon of dried Lavender (*Lavandula* spp.)
- » 1 teaspoon of dried Heartsease petals (*Viola tricolor*)

- » 20 drops of Lavender essential oil
- » 1 teaspoon of sweet almond oil
- » a mixing bowl
- » a wooden spoon
- » a cupcake mould

The Spell

Make sure everything is completely dry before beginning, including your hands, tools and work area. If not, you will end up with your bath bomb going off too early!

Mix together the bicarbonate of soda, citric acid, Lavender and Heartsease petals in the bowl with the wooden spoon and say:

Bath delight,

Soon to bubble,

Soon comes the night,

Then release my troubles.

Add the Lavender essential oil and sweet almond oil and mix with the spoon until well combined. Spoon into the cupcake mould. Leave to set at room temperature in a cool, dry place (will depend on weather) and then unmould. Use straight away or store by sealing well in foil and keeping in a dry, dark and cool place.

Pop into a warm bath while the water is running.

To get the most out of your bath, make sure you unplug and let go: turn off your phone, dim the lights, perhaps play some relaxing soft music – and you might even like to light a lovely Lavender or pink Rose candle.

Nightmares usually occur because you have not unwound from the worries and concerns of the day. This spell will help by creating a relaxing bath experience to release your negative or unwanted thoughts while soothing your way to a pleasant night's sleep.

If you dream of Faeries, they could have a message for you, so listen well. It can also mean you need to follow your own intuition more closely at the moment. If you are chasing or following a Faerie in the dream, it means that you need to follow your heart.

Aziza Faerie Study Spell

This spell will create a lovely herbal pouch for you to tuck into your pocket, leave on your desk or take with you to class. The herbs are all selected for their study-support powers and you will be aligning yourself with the Aziza Faeries of Africa, who are not only wisdom keepers but also love passing knowledge on to humans who are keen to learn.

Timings
Waxing Moon, Wednesday, Late Night

Find and Gather

- » a fluorite crystal
- » a small drawstring pouch or bag – something you don't mind carrying with you
- » an African Violet flower (*Saintpaulia ionantha*)
- » a whole Walnut (*Juglans* spp.)
- » a Sage stick or incense (*Salvia officinalis*)
- » a violet-coloured candle
- » matches
- » a small piece of cooked Sweet Potato (*Yam*) (*Ipomoea batatas*)

The Spell

This spell is more effective when cast outside. Spread out all your spell ingredients, light your candle and say:

Light of Aziza,

Shine on me now,

Please share your wisdom freely,

Graciously I bow.

Light your Sage; this is to cleanse the area but also to inspire the gaining of wisdom.

Pop the Walnut and the fluorite crystal in your pouch, pass it through the Sage smoke and say:

My mind will receive,

My mind will retain.

Now add the African Violet to the pouch and say:

For you, wise Faeries,

I thank you for light,

For learning and knowledge,

You share from this night.

Pass the pouch through the smoke three more times.

Take the Sweet Potato and bury it in the ground, and say:

Thank you again,

For you and the Earth.

The Aziza are thought to have given humans life-saving knowledge and wisdom. They are also said to have taught us how to cook Sweet Potato, how to extract oils from Palm tree nuts and most importantly, how to use plants medicinally.

African Violets are not violets at all; their species name, *ionantha*, means 'with flowers like violets'. They will promote higher learning and a deeper connection spiritually while also offering protection.

Oosood Faerie New Baby Spell

*The Oosood are Siberian Faeries only visible to new babies and their
mothers for the first week after birth. They will offer insight about the
future of the child and also confer their blessings upon the baby. Use this
spell for yourself or create for another family member or friend. Ensure
that the mother leaves the gift out and writes her own note of gratitude.
Perhaps include a pen, paper and a note on how to do this.*

Timings

Waxing Moon, Monday,
Morning

Find and Gather

» a small and beautiful basket
» a beautiful floral napkin or
scarf
» a collection of pastel ribbons
– length is dependent on
size of basket
» very small flowers
» tiny biscuits
» little fruit-flavoured sweets
» berries
» pen and paper or a card

The Spell

Line the basket with the floral napkin or scarf.

Decorate the basket with the ribbons and anything else you feel you would like.

Place the treats inside and say:

Oosood Faerie,

Caring and good,

These treats are for you.

On your piece of paper or in your card, in your own words, thank the Oosood for their presence and blessings and tuck it into the basket.

Place the flowers in the basket and say,

With thanks and with love,

I am grateful for your presence.

Leave the basket outside your front door or just inside it. Whatever is left after a week, take to a large, long-living tree and bury in the earth.

New mothers, who themselves receive gifts of flowers and food treats from their visitors, create and leave these types of gifts for the Oosood to ensure good blessings and favourable predictions about their child.

The three good Faeries in the *Sleeping Beauty* fairytale are thought to have derived from stories of the Siberian Oosood as they bring gifts and prophecy just as the Oosood do.

Brownie Strawberry Flower Gratitude Spell

*Brownies are a type of Faerie that like to live closely with humans and are
generally very helpful around the home. They will come out of their hiding
places at night to do or complete chores around the home. Your Brownies
will return to their hiding places before the dawn breaks. Care must be
taken because if you are not respectful of them they will quickly turn into
unfriendly Boggarts and with that, bad luck will fall upon your home. It is
very important to show your gratitude regularly and never ever make fun
of them or speak ill of them.*

Timings

New Moon, Monday, Evening

Find and Gather

» a small slice of cake

» a spoonful of honey

» a few Strawberry flowers
(*Fragaria* spp.) – if you
can't find flowers, then a few strawberries will do

» milk

» a beautiful flower-patterned plate (*to be used only for this purpose*)

» a beautiful bowl (*to be used only for this purpose*)

The Spell

I do this spell each New Moon to keep my Brownies happy and to let them know how grateful I am of their assistance and work.

Put the plate in a central place in your home, preferably the kitchen, dining or lounge room.

On the plate, arrange the cake with care, drizzle it with the honey and say:

Lovely good Brownies,

To thank you, here are things to eat,

Sweet cake and honey treats.

Place the Strawberry flowers or strawberries around the cake and say:

Flowers of purity, love and humility,

I give to you with my very deep gratitude.

Fill the bowl with milk, then hold it above the cake plate, saying:

Drink, good Brownies,

And I toast your good deeds.

Place the bowl of milk next to the cake.

In the morning bury what remains on the plate and bowl in the garden.

If, for some reason, you do anger your Brownies and they turn to Boggarts, then they can be placated by hanging a horseshoe above your front door and placing a plate of salt on the doorstep for a night.

A new lover is on the near horizon for those who dream of strawberries, and dreaming of strawberries is particularly good for those about to wed, as it foretells a very good and happy marriage.

Attract Faerie Friends Spell

Faeries love to find special private places that they can call their own and
if you can create one for them, you might just find that they move right in.
This spell will help you create and dedicate such a place, a tiny grotto in
your garden or even in your home.

Timings
Waxing Moon, Wednesday, Daytime

Find and Gather
» a collection of small treasures
  (*such as stones, crystals, shells,*
  plants, ribbons, bells, windchimes,
  flowers)
» 1 pink and 1 green candle
» a few tablespoons of wine in a
  tiny glass
» a small piece of cake
» a saucer
» a bunch of Thyme (*Thymus*
  vulgaris)
» matches

The Spell

Create a small space in your garden or perhaps you could set up in a corner of your home. Perhaps a bookcase shelf or a lovely old open wooden box could be used. As long as it is somewhere that is to be dedicated as a home for Faeries and nothing else. Decorate it with all the lovely treasures you have collected. Place the pink candle on one side of this Faerie grotto and the green on the other, light and say:

> *Welcome Faerie folk,*
> *You may make this your home.*
> *But only the good,*
> *May stop as they roam.*

Place the wine and cake next to the entrance and say:

> *I offer you shelter,*
> *I offer you treats.*
> *My promise to tend you,*
> *I will always keep.*

Decorate the grotto with springs of Thyme. Make sure you do keep your promise and keep the grotto clean and tidy and feed your Faeries with milk, honey, bread and cakes. If you fail to do so they will move on.

Ensure that you leave offerings at the Full Moon, at the change of season and on celebratory days. They will love treats of sparkling and still wine, special cakes, sweets and thoughtful little gifts at these times.

Faeries love Thyme, but so do bees! You would be well advised to plant Thyme or place a small pot of Thyme next to your grotto for your Faeries. 'Thyme' means 'courage and strength' and Ancient Greek and Roman soldiers would bathe in water infused with Thyme to boost their bravery and energy.

Pixie Increase Circle of Friends Spell

This infused oil is perfect to decant into a roll-on bottle to carry with you. Pixies are found through mythology, folklore and literature. They are sometimes wingless little folk who love to party and dance and adore playing with children. Those hailing from the western regions of England have the pointed ears and hats that some may be familiar with.

Timings
Waxing Moon, Friday, Morning

Find and Gather

- » ¼ cup dried Dill (*Anethum graveolens*)
- » ¼ cup dried pink Roses (*Rosa* spp.)
- » ¼ cup dried Lemongrass (*Cymbopogon citratus*)
- » a gorgeous sterilised jar with a lid
- » sweet almond oil – amount will depend on jar size

The Spell
Place the dried Dill in the jar and say:
> *Herb of luck,*
> *Of protection.*

Add the dried Roses to the jar and say:

Flower of friendship,

And healing hearts.

Place the Lemongrass in the jar and say:

Herb of binding,

Friendships bright.

Pour in the oil to cover.

Put the lid on, shake well to combine and then swirl in a circular motion while saying:

Circle of friends expand and grow,

There is a space,

And this is a place.

New friends welcome,

New friends come,

Together the circle grows.

Leave in a cool, dry, dark place for two weeks, visiting daily and repeating the shaking, the circular motion and the chant.

Pass through a fine sieve if you are using in a roll-on bottle.

You can dab this oil on yourself or on places where you wish friendships to form and grow. You can also dab on objects you use in community get-togethers (such as tables, chairs and even candles that you may burn.)

Dill will help any of your friendship gatherings stay safe from evil and negative influences. Hanging sprigs around doorways is one way to ensure this but you could also use this oil.

Lemongrass has the supposed curious power to keep snakes out of your garden if planted near the boundaries. It can also increase psychic powers and is a very good friendship booster.

FAERIE BEAUTY
AND
SPA SPELLS

Chamomile Faerie Morning Dew Spell

This spell will help you bring your inner beauty out with the rising sun. It also sooths and balances the skin and mind with the blessings of the lovely Faeries who care and love Chamomile flowers. It is preferable that you use fresh flowers and herbs for this spell. Be sure to collect your morning dew from plants that are organically grown and are non-toxic.

Timings
Full Moon, Sunday, Dawn

Find and Gather
- » 1 tablespoon of morning dew
- » 1 tablespoon of fresh Chamomile (*Matricaria chamomilla*)
- » 1 tablespoon of fresh Thyme (*Thymus vulgaris*)
- » 4 tablespoons of apple cider vinegar
- » 2 slices of lemon (*Citrus × limon*)
- » 2 cups of rainwater
- » a piece of cheesecloth or muslin
- » string
- » a saucepan
- » a large heat-proof bowl
- » a large towel
- » cold water

The Spell

Take the Chamomile and Thyme and place in the centre of the cloth and, sprinkling with the morning dew, say:

Soft as the dew,

Fresh as the plant.

Beauty and balance,

With grace please grant.

Tie up the cloth to make a little bag, securing the herbs inside.

In your saucepan, bring the water and apple cider vinegar to the boil. Turn off heat, add the herb bag and the lemon slices. Cover and leave to steep for 10 minutes.

Pour into your bowl and place on a table. Place the towel over your head and lean over the bowl with your face about 30 cm (12") above the water.

Relax and visualise a walk at dawn with the Chamomile Faeries and focus on the equilibrium, relaxation, energy, love and support they impart. Stay as long as you feel comfortable.

Be sure to splash your face well with cold water to close your pores and keep all the Faerie goodness inside.

The mixture and any discards created while making this spell should be buried in the earth with thanks to the Faeries after use.

You might like to retain the mixture after your facial steam and add to a bath as Chamomile in a bath is said to attract love to you. Washing your hands with Chamomile will bring money your way so you may like to use it for this too!

Morning dew is very magickal and, collected during certain moon phases or special days, will impart the particular energy of these to the general healing and restorative powers of water collected at dawn from flowers and their plants. The dew of Midsummer, when the powers of the morning dew are strongest, is considered especially precious.

Faerie Queen Titania Summer Bronzer

The Faerie Queen Titania brings the warmth of life, encourages our individual expression and helps us to stay young, happy and appreciating the sweetness of life. You will find this recipe creates a fantastic skin bronzer that you can use to impart a sunny glow to your face and body. You can use it to contour too. This botanical pot of make-up goodness also magickly captures the warmth, power and energy of the Sun for a really good boost when feeling at all flat or unsure of yourself.

Timings
Full Moon, Sunday, Late Afternoon/Evening

Find and Gather

- » sprigs of Thyme (*Thymus vulgaris*)
- » 2 teaspoons tapioca flour
- » powdered Cacao (*Theobroma cacao*)
- » ground Turmeric (*Curcuma longa*)
- » ground Nutmeg (*Myristica fragrans*)
- » a bowl
- » some very small bowls
- » a wooden spoon
- » a sterilised jar and lid
- » a round makeup powder brush
- » a gold cloth large enough to sit your mixing bowl on
- » a mirror

The Spell

Place all your tools and ingredients on the gold cloth. You want the setting sun to fall on you and particularly on your mixing bowl if possible. Place the sprigs of Thyme around the mixing bowl.

Add your tapioca flour and 2 teaspoons of Cacao to the bowl and while mixing, say:

Sun, look down now with your strength and power,

Add all your gifts right here in the flour.

Queen Titania, Faerie divine.

Your happy sweet love,

Could you please here entwine.

The next part will be up to you. Take out about a teaspoon of the mixture and place in one of the small bowls. Add Turmeric and Nutmeg (separately or combined) and mix until you create a colour you like.

When you are happy, mix your desired shade in the large bowl of the tapioca flour mixture, matching it to your sample. Be sure to write down your mixture amounts so you can recreate it. While you are stirring the larger mixture, say again:

Sun, look down now with your strength and power,

Add all your gifts right here in the flour.

Once finished, place your bronzer in the jar and store in a cool, dry place. Will keep up to eight months. Those who prefer a red tint to their bronzer may like to experiment with a little beetroot powder as well.

The best time to create this would be during the Summer Solstice. The Faeries are also out to celebrate so make sure you place a bowl of cream and a plate of honey cake out to encourage them to join you.

Titania is the queen of the Faeries in William Shakespeare's play *A Midsummer Night's Dream*.

Apple Faerie Sweet Words Lip Balm

*Faeries do appreciate love and the truth. Apples are known to help purify
your emotions and let you have a better understanding of the Fae. Their
inclusion in this very soothing and lovely lip balm will help you say what
is in your heart, sweetly and with purity. For some Faerie sparkle, you can
add a little cake decorating glitter or pearlescent dust.*

Timings
Full Moon, Tuesday, Morning

Find and Gather

» 1 tablespoon of coconut oil
» 1 tablespoon of coconut butter
» 1 teaspoon of vitamin E oil
» 3 apple (*Malus domestica*) spice herbal
  teabags
» ¼ teaspoon of raw sugar
» ¼ teaspoon of Vanilla extract (*Vanilla
  planifolia*)
» 2 tablespoons of beeswax pellets
» a double boiler or alternative
» a wooden spoon
» 1 or 2 tiny sterilised containers
  suitable for lip balm

The Spell

Fill the outer double boiler with water up to the half-way mark. Heat gently but do not allow to simmer or boil.

Add the coconut oil, coconut butter and vitamin E oil to the inner vessel and while stirring with the wooden spoon, say:

Soft and smooth oils combine,

A lovely lip balm will soon be mine.

Now add the apple teabags, raw sugar and Vanilla extract and keep stirring while saying:

Apples pure, loving and kind,

Let the words that I say be sweet,

And unbind.

Take off heat and leave to steep for 5 minutes. Once cool enough to handle, gently squeeze the teabags into the mixture then remove. Place back on the heat and add the beeswax pellets. Stir until melted and well combined. Pour into containers for use.

To use: Spread a little on your lips.

Apples, and in particular the apple tree, are symbols of fertility in Celtic mythology and are used in spells to assist in conception and love spells. Eating the first apple of the season could ensure that you would conceive and having a pregnant woman eat such fruit would ensure a good crop that year.

The Faeries love apples so they are very good offerings for them. To encourage Faeries to your Midsummer celebrations or at other times that you would like their company, try burning apple-tree bark incense.

The Sidhe Elixir of Youth Spell

The Sidhe are a noble race of Faeries descended from the Tuatha dé Danann, who are still thought to live in Ireland today. The secret of youth is said to be one of their many held wisdoms and this elixir spell will help you create a gorgeous rich beauty oil of rejuvenation.

Timings
Full Moon, Friday, Morning

Find and Gather

- » a perfect red Rose (*Rosa* spp.) with at least 4 cm (2") of stem left on
- » 8 tablespoons of almond oil
- » 3 tablespoons of vitamin E oil
- » 8 drops of Rose essential oil
- » a beautiful piece of green tourmaline crystal
- » cheesecloth or muslin cloth
- » a gorgeous sterilised glass jar and lid
- » a large, deep glass bowl
- » a bowl with the capacity of your jar
- » spring water or rainwater
- » 3 sticks, about 8 cm (4") each in length
- » string or wire

The Spell

Place the red Rose and the oils into the glass jar, seal with lid and place your green tourmaline crystal on top of the lid. Say the following:

I ask that the Sidhe,

Gentry of land,

Take my mixture at hand.

Place your jar in the large glass bowl and fill with water up to about a quarter of the height of the jar. Put it all in a cool, dry place where it can remain undisturbed for three days and say:

Beautiful folk,

The secrets of youth,

For me please uncloak.

After three days, take the jar out and strain the oil into another fresh bowl and then pour the oil without the Rose back into the original jar. Take the Rose and bind two sticks to the stems to emulate legs. Cross the other stick under the Rose so it looks like arms. Place it in the large bowl of water and say:

I offer you this for this blessing of youth,

A sacrifice made for you and your truth.

Then bury the Rose figure in a very lovely place in the garden.

Every seven years a lake named Lough Gur in Ireland drains and the entrance to the land of perpetual youth, 'Tir na nÓg', is revealed. The land around the lake is a place that the Sidhe are very fond of and where they can be found. Although they will allow mortals in, one Faerie known as Beanne Fhionn once abducted a mortal to take to Faerieland but not before drowning them in the lake, so caution must be taken in case it happens again.

As well as having healing and magick properties, Green tourmaline crystal is a strong conductor of plant energy so will increase the power of plant energy.

Faerie Rejuvenating Milk Bath Spell

One of the best offerings you can share with Faeries is milk; they adore it. Make sure you pour a little of this bath onto the ground for the Faeries before you hop in. Rosebuds are included in this gorgeous self-love bath to impart beauty, boost your passionate side and look after your self-confidence. Lavender is one of the great relaxers and balancers, but it is also a very effective energy cleanser. Step into this bath to rid yourself of the negative energy seen and unseen, and to rejuvenate your mind, body and soul.

Timings
Full Moon/Any Day, Evening

Find and Gather

- » 1 handful of dried Rosebuds (*Rosa* spp.)
- » 2 heaped tablespoons of dried Lavender (*Lavandula* spp.)
- » 1 cup of boiling water
- » 2 cups of coconut milk
- » 1 cup of cow's milk
- » 1 tablespoon of honey
- » a large heat-proof glass bowl
- » a few lovely scented candles
- » a lidded glass jar

The Spell

Add the Rosebuds and Lavender to the large glass bowl. Pour the boiling water over the top and say:

> *Flowers of Faerie,*
>
> *Flowers delight.*
>
> *Lie here and mingle,*
>
> *For all of the night.*

Leave overnight to steep.

The next day, stir in the coconut milk and the cow's milk, and say:

> *Milk of the land,*
>
> *Here by my hand,*
>
> *Renewed I shall be.*

Drizzle in the honey and say:

> *Sweetness and light.*

You can store this mixture in the glass jar in the fridge for two days. To use, pour into a nice warm bath. You may like to strain it if you don't like the idea of the flowers in your bath, or you might actually like to add more! Light your candles, grab a good book, put on some relaxing music and enjoy this rejuvenating bath.

Throughout the United Kingdom and Ireland, the preferred offering for Faeries is milk, sometimes sweetened with honey. In Ireland especially it is believed in many places that failure to leave out a little milk on the doorstep regularly will make local Faeries angry and lead them to play tricks or even start stealing.

Lavender brings love along with its calming and purifying properties. Cleopatra, along with being famous for her milk baths, was also very partial to Lavender-based perfumes.

Moss Maiden Face Mask Spell

*Of German origin, the Moss Maidens are very beautiful and friendly
Faeries who spin and weave moss around the forest floor. Here you
will create a rejuvenating face mask that honours the work these Faeries
do and in place of moss, use green tea. Banana, coconut cream and
honey will help add a moisturising boost while the green tea will offer
rejuvenating properties.*

Timings

Waxing Moon, Sunday, Afternoon/Evening

Find and Gather

- » 1 tablespoon of green tea-leaves
  (*Camellia sinensis*)
- » ¼ cup of water
- » I teaspoon of mashed banana
- » 1 teaspoon of organic honey
- » 1 teaspoon of thick coconut
  cream
- » a small saucepan
- » a cup
- » a bowl
- » a fine strainer

The Spell

Place the green tea-leaves in the saucepan and cover with water. Bring to a vigorous boil and then turn off heat and cover. Leave for ten minutes to steep. Uncover and leave to cool completely, then using the strainer, strain the green tea into the cup. Mix together the mashed banana, coconut cream and honey very well and say:

Fruit and honey,

Moss green tea,

Faerie sweet maidens,

Caring and beauty share me.

Add as much green tea water as you need to make a nice paste.

Apply to your face, avoiding the eye and lip areas, and leave for 20 minutes. Rest somewhere (maybe in a cool darker place in the garden) and visualise the beautiful Moss Maidens, spinning their moss and helping you achieve a glowing, soothed and rejuvenated skin. Rinse in cool clear water and pat your face gently dry.

Take any leftover face mask, the green tea-leaves and any other plant matter left and bury in a dark place in your garden giving thanks to the Moss Maidens.

Green tea is created from *Camellia sinensis*, the same plant that gives us black tea. The leaves in green tea do not undergo the oxidation process of other teas and so contain a far greater percentage of health-beneficial antioxidants.

The Moss Maidens live in the roots of large trees in dense forests and are said to hold the healing wisdom of all the plants of the world.

Ijósálfar Fae Face Mist Spell

Some Swedish elves that are thought of as Faeries who are light, beautiful and rather good, live in the sky. They are known as one race of the Alver and are known as the Ijósálfar. The other race are not so lovely; they are thought of as bad and live within the earth. This race of Alver are called the Døkkálfar. This face mist is inspired by the Ijósálfar and will impart a refreshing boost not only to your skin but to your mood as well. Soothing, uplifting and refreshing.

Timings
Full Moon, Friday, Morning

Find and Gather

- » ¼ cup of Orange Blossom (*Citrus × sinensis*) water
- » ¾ cup of spring water
- » 2 tablespoons of Aloe Vera (*Aloe vera*) juice
- » 1 teaspoon of pure Vanilla extract (*Vanilla planifolia*)
- » a glass mixing bowl
- » a wooden spoon
- » a sterilised glass spray bottle

The Spell

With the wooden spoon, mix the Orange Blossom water and spring water together in the bowl and say:

> *Sweet waters of orange,*
>
> *Of fresh running springs,*
>
> *Mix with the air around me,*
>
> *and uplifting goodness bring.*

Add the Aloe Vera juice and say:

> *Soothing and healing,*
>
> *Bless this mix with good feelings.*

Add the Vanilla extract and say:

> *Perfume and sweeten,*
>
> *Negativity beaten.*

Decant into your glass spray bottle and spritz all over your face as needed. Store in the fridge for up to 4 months.

The very best replacement for wine, mead or any alcoholic beverage in spells is orange juice or a dash of Orange Blossom water in a glass of water. Oranges are considered pure, lucky and chaste, so they can not only be trusted but also bring good fortune.

J.R.R. Tolkien is said to have been inspired by the Ijósálfar when creating the wise elven race in his Lord of the Rings books.

Ginger Faerie Sugar Scrub Spell

This zesty body scrub will lift your energy for the day and is very good if you are feeling flat, experiencing negative feelings or are weighed down with challenges. It will give you a zippy and uplifting morning start. Ginger will bring you the energies of clarity, courage and determination while providing tension relief. Lemon helps clear negative thoughts, and clears and cleanses while adding zest to your day. Fairies who look after Ginger plants are warm and loving and display great determination.

Timings
Waning Moon, Tuesday, Morning

Find and Gather

- » 1 cup of cane sugar
- » ½ cup coconut oil
- » 2 teaspoons of ground Ginger (*Zingiber officinale*)
- » 1 teaspoon of lemon zest (*Citrus × limon*)
- » a bowl
- » a spoon
- » a sterilised jar and lid

The Spell

Place the sugar, coconut oil, ground Ginger and lemon zest in the bowl and mix until all combined while saying:

Starting the day,

With you, Ginger Fae.

Lemon for zest,

This day to be best.

Scoop into the jar and keep in a cool dry place for three months, or up to six months in the fridge.

To use: with a clean, dry tablespoon, stir to ensure ingredients are combined. While in the shower, place a good heaped tablespoonful in your hand and massage onto your body in a circular motion. More can be used as needed.

While using, say:

This day I awake,

This day I face with renewed energy.

This day I am blessed,

This day I awake.

Rinse well but don't use soap as this will strip away the beneficial oils and botanicals.

Ginger is a plant that can bring an increase in finances and resources. Try sprinkling ground Ginger in your wallet or purse. Any spell can be given extra power and a boost by the addition of Ginger.

Try tying an orange ribbon around the jar of your Ginger Body Scrub Spell mix. Colour magick can also help draw in the energies you desire. Orange corresponds with action, joy, speed and success.

Daisy Faerie Feet Foot Soak Spell

If you have been standing for long hours and are suffering from sore, aching feet or you are feeling weighed down with troubles, this foot soak will give you some relief and have you stepping as lightly as a Faerie. The inclusion of energising essential oils and fresh, happiness-inspiring Daisies will impart peace of mind, protection and support.

Timings
Full Moon, Monday, Midday

Find and Gather
» ½ cup Himalayan salt
» ½ cup Epsom salt
» 3 drops Peppermint (*Mentha × piperita*) essential oil
» 3 drops Eucalyptus (*Eucalyptus* spp.) essential oil
» a small handful of dried English Daisies (*Bellis perennis*)
» a large glass bowl
» a wooden spoon
» sterilised glass jar/s

The Spell

Mix together the salts and essential oils in the large glass bowl with the wooden spoon. As you do, say:

Step out lightly and step out sweet,

The heaviness lifts away from my feet.

Sprinkle the Daisies over the salts, mix through and say:

Happy little flowers,

Bright, calm and lovely.

Daisy Faerie, thank you,

For helping my recovery.

Pack into glass jar/s and seal tightly. Store in a cool, dry place.

To use, add 3 heaped tablespoons to a warm foot bath.

You may like to add a few fresh daisies as well.

There are many folklore stories, especially throughout the United Kingdom, that Faeries steal human babies, leaving their own offspring in their place. To shrink the human infants down to Faerie size, they would feed them daisies.

All mints have been used throughout time to attract wealth and prosperity. Peppermint oil will remove negativity from wooden furniture and floors if you add to a polishing carrier oil or even to water you are cleaning with.

Calendula Faerie Hair Repair Spell

Wash your bad hair days and negativity away with this gorgeous nourishing shampoo. This mixture will cleanse, repair and protect your hair while adding a little extra magick to your day. Calendula flowers offer healing, protection and release — most important when you are seeking to rid yourself of a condition or unwanted energy. The addition of Thyme assists in connecting with Faeries, Rosemary is for clarity and revival, and Rose will impart beauty.

Timings
Waxing/Full Moon, Thursday, Midday

Find and Gather
» ½ cup of dried Calendula flowers (*Calendula officinalis*)
» 2 cups of boiling distilled water
» ¼ cup of liquid Castile (*vegetable based*) soap
» 4 drops of Thyme (*Thymus vulgaris*) essential oil
» 4 drops of Rosemary (*Rosmarinus officinalis*) essential oil
» 4 drops of Rose (*Rosa* spp.) essential oil
» a large heat-proof glass or ceramic bowl
» a wooden spoon

» a fine strainer

» a beautiful sterilised glass bottle with lid

» a funnel (*optional*)

The Spell

Put the Calendula flowers into the large bowl and then pour in the boiling water. Stir and say:

Sunny gold flowers,

Of healing delight.

Impart your wonderful powers,

So lovely and bright.

Leave for at least 30 minutes or until completely cool.

Add the Castile soap and the essential oils. Stir well and say:

Oils of herbs, plants and flowers,

Mix together all your powers.

Pour into the glass bottle, keep out of direct sunlight and use within six weeks.

To use: shake well and use as you would your regular shampoo.

You would be right in thinking that the name 'Calendula' is related to the word 'calendar'. It springs from the Latin *calends*, meaning the first day of each month, because Calendulas flower throughout the year in many places.

Calendula flowers are empowered by the sun, so to benefit fully from their gifts they must be picked at midday. Daytime is also the best time to harness their magickal powers for creating and casting calendula-based spells.

FAERIE
HAPPINESS AND
WISH SPELLS

Sage Faerie Remove Negativity Spell

This zesty and earthy shower powder will remove negative energy incredibly effectively with the added magick of Sage Faerie assistance. Lavender will not only impart a gorgeous fragrance but will offer protection along with cleansing. Rolled oats and kaolin white clay powder will leave your skin soft and calmed. Use when you have had a heavy energy day, are feeling under attack or want to cleanse your physical and etherical body before a ritual or event.

Timings
Waning Moon, Saturday, Midnight

Find and Gather
» 2 tablespoons of dried Sage
   (*Salvia officinalis*)
» 2 tablespoons of dried Lavender
   (*Lavandula* spp.)
» ½ cup of rolled oats
» 4 tablespoons of lemon zest
» ½ cup of tea-leaves
» ½ cup of kaolin white clay powder
» a coffee/spice grinder
» a mixing bowl
» a wooden spoon
» a sterilised jar and lid

The Spell

Grind the Sage, Lavender, oats, lemon zest and tea in the grinder and mill until you have a fine mixture. Place in the mixing bowl and add the kaolin white clay powder. Mix really well while saying:

Flowers, herbs, earth and fruit,

Together mix well and negativity boot.

Faerie of Sage,

Clear all who will use,

Of negative energy,

And make all anew.

Store in the jar and use within six months.

To use: use in the shower. Sprinkle into your hands or onto a buffer and massage well into your skin, then rinse away. When using, make sure you focus on all the negative energy washing off you and down the drain.

Never grow Sage alone in a garden bed as it is considered very unlucky. Grow other plants with it for company, especially Rosemary, as they get on well and encourage each other to grow.

The practice of bathing or showering to rid oneself of negative energies is as old as time. Water naturally lifts more than just surface dirt: it will wash away toxic feelings and the heaviness of events and negative thoughts. You are left with your own personal energy and aura free and clear.

Leprechaun Good Luck in Business Spell

To invite some luck from the Leprechauns will most likely bring a bit of prankster behaviour as well but, if you are like me, you might find this energy uplifting. They are not malicious but they do like to play tricks and if you can appreciate their humour you may find they reward you. This spell uses Clover, the plant of their land, and if you are already lucky enough to possess a four-leafed one, by all means include it in this spell. Bay leaves are also used as they are very good at attracting reward for merit.

Timings
Waxing Moon, Thursday, Daytime

Find and Gather

» music, preferably fiddle, tin whistle or pipes
» an orange candle
» a small green bag
» 3 gold coins
» 3 Clover leaves (*Trifolium* spp.)
» 3 Bay leaves (*Laurus nobilis*)
» a gold ribbon 30 cm (*12"*) in length
» salt
» a joke

The Spell

In your place of business, play your selected music, light the orange candle and say:

> *Light of joy, of abundance and luck,*
> *I promise to work as hard as the Leprechaun,*
> *And in happiness I trust.*

Place your gold coins, Clover leaves and Bay leaves in the green bag and say:

> *Gold attract gold,*
> *Bay bring success,*
> *Clover the luck,*
> *So that I do my best.*

Sprinkle the salt over and say:

> *Salt of the ground,*
> *Balance and protect.*

Tie the bag with the gold ribbon and hang it in your place of business – somewhere you can see it but it won't be disturbed. Read out your joke, blow out the candle but retain to use again for this spell if you need to redo it at a later date. If for any reason any bad luck befalls you, place one of the gold coins on your doorstep with milk and cake. Redo the whole spell.

Without a doubt the most industrious of the Faeries, Leprechauns usually work as cobblers and tailors. It is said that all Leprechauns own a pot of gold and that if you catch one, he has to give it to you. However it is nearly impossible to do this, as Leprechauns are consummate tricksters and incredibly smart.

Clover fields attract Faeries, so are good places to visit if you are hoping to see them. Not only will a four-leaf Clover attract luck, but it will break any Faerie spell as well and offer protection from Faeries who may wish to do you harm.

Faerie Art Divination Spell

Faeries love art and creativity so this divination spell using crayons will hold great appeal for them. Check with a tea-leaf reading book or an online resource for an extensive list of shapes and symbols and their meanings, but I am sure you will recognise elements from the abstract art you create that will make sense to you personally. Open your heart, listen to your soul and lean in to hear those Faerie whispers, too!

Timings

New Moon, Monday, Late Night

Find and Gather

»   a collection of crayons

»   a kitchen grater

»   baking paper (*greaseproof paper*)

»   tiny dried flowers and/or petals

»   brown paper

»   paper towels

»   a clothing iron

* The quantities used in this spell will depend on the size of the artwork and how many you wish to create.

The Spell

Although you can use any size paper to create this divination artwork, start by cutting/tearing 2 pieces, each about the size of an A4 sheet of paper.

Select a few crayons in the colours that you feel most drawn to.

Heat your iron to the 'Cotton' setting (or little less than the highest setting).

Using the kitchen grater, grate a crayon until you have about a teaspoon of gratings and place on one sheet of the baking paper. Repeat with each crayon you have selected and place wherever you wish on the paper, leaving a gap of about 2 cm (1") between the little piles of gratings.

Once complete, sprinkle the dried whole flowers or petals over your colourful gratings.

Cover with the second piece of baking paper. Place a few sheets of brown paper on top and press with the iron. As you do, say:

Faeries of future,
Faeries my plea,
Let's mix these colours,
And see what is to be.

Remove the brown paper and then peel off the top sheet of baking paper. Your Faerie art reading will be revealed. This can be mounted onto a sturdier piece of paper (you may need to use glue), or you can keep it in a journal. Be sure to write your reading and date alongside it.

Try adding herbs, leaves and other small treasures to your Faerie divination artwork. It can be very interesting to match the energies of flowers and herbs to the divination you are seeking. For a love reading, use red or yellow Roses or even Carnations. For healing, Calendula and white Roses, and for messages from the other side perhaps Lilies.

Divination using this method is akin to 'carromancy', the art of divination using melting wax. You are also using 'anthomancy' if you add flowers, which is divination using flowers, and even chartomancy, using things on paper to see the future.

Bergamot Faerie Stop Worry Linen Spray

This spell asks the Faeries to help bring the full power of two precious essential oils to life in a refreshing, worry-releasing linen spray. Bergamot helps induce a restful sleep by relieving tension and anxiety, and for those in warmer climates, it also serves as a very effective insect repellant at night. Ylang-ylang releases negative emotions and uplifts the spirit while calming and relaxing body and mind.

Timings
Waning, Monday, Midnight/Dusk

Find and Gather

» ¼ cup of rain or spring water – approx. amount to fill your selected spray bottle
» 4 drops of Bergamot (*Citrus bergamia*) essential oil
» 4 drops of Ylang-ylang (*Cananga odorata*) essential oil
» 1 tablespoon of rubbing alcohol
» a small sterilised glass spray bottle – larger than ¼ cup in size

The Spell

You may find you need to adjust your measurements of each ingredient depending on the size of the spray bottle. You can always make up this amount or double in a lidded mixing jar, shake and then decant into smaller glass spray bottles.

To your bottle/mixing bottle, add your water and say:

Hold my emotions,

Water of Life.

Soothe them,

Calm them,

And relieve all my strife.

Add the essential oils and say:

Faerie laughter,

Lift my heart,

Help me see,

The way from dark.

Add the rubbing alcohol and shake well.

To use: Shake well and then spritz lightly on your bedlinen before retiring for the evening.

Store in a cool, dry place. Keeps for up to 6 months.

Bergamot is also very good at bringing stability if you are feeling mentally and emotionally out of balance and is also used as a natural antidepressant. Earl Grey tea is black tea flavoured with Bergamot oil.

There are many folklore stories that tell of Faeries who watch children as they sleep and whisper stories, fables and Faerie tales to them. It's said that children who have listened well can recount them afterwards.

Tuatha dé Danann Creativity Spell

The Tuatha dé Danann are said to be the ancestors of the Irish race and although they are firmly entwined with the stories of Faeries right to the current day, there is much debate about whether they were Faeries, gods or a type of superhuman. There is also disagreement about whether they were completely benign. However they have always been synonymous with healing, magick and the arts. This spell will bring the good of the Tuatha dé Danann to you and help to remove a creative block, make artistic skills easier to acquire and fill your world with inspirations.

Timings
Waxing Moon, Friday, Morning

Find and Gather

- » 1 cup of spring or rain water
- » dragon's blood incense
- » a good handful of Clover leaves (*Trifolium* spp.)
- » 4 Clover blossoms (*can be dried*)
- » a sprig of Rosemary (*Rosmarinus officinalis*)
- » 8 drops of Rosemary essential oil
- » a small tigers eye crystal, small enough to fit into misting bottle
- » a large, wide glass bowl

- » a fine strainer
- » a sterilised glass jar with lid
- » a glass misting/spray bottle
- » 2 tablespoons of glycerin

The Spell

Find a lovely sun-filled spot out in Nature or your garden. Fill your glass bowl with the spring or rainwater and then set your bowl upon the earth so that the sun can shine brightly on the water. Light the dragon's blood incense and pass the smoke over all your gathered items.

Drop the Clover flowers and leaves into the water and say:

Sweet plant of the Emerald Isle,

Lovely and true,

Let us welcome the Tuatha dé Danann,

In light for me as for you.

Drop in the Rosemary sprig and say:

Artful memory,

Always be true.

Place the tiger's eye crystal in the water and say:

Stone of creative light,

Guide through the night.

Leave out in the sunlight for an hour then strain into the glass jar and add glycerin and store in a cool dry place.

To use: decant into a glass misting bottle and spray into the air around you when you want to boost creative energy.

Rosemary is an excellent Faerie herb to bring into any studio space as it promotes memory and clarity and connects you with what you have learned and what is going on in the here and now.

Tiger's eye crystal will help you turn ideas into reality, especially artistic and creative ones. It also promotes good fortune and helps boost optimism.

Seelie Dandelion Wish Spell

The Seelie are good Faeries of the British Isles who are known to help humans and also bless people who have assisted them with rewards. They travel on the winds and are very beautiful, light-hearted fae-folk who are known to play tricks. I'm sure you have picked a Dandelion and blown the seeds, closed your eyes and made a wish. This tradition comes to us from the Faeries. In spreading the seeds of the Dandelion plant, we are helping the Faeries and in doing so, they in turn may grant us a wish.

Timings
Waxing Moon, Sunday, Daytime

Find and Gather

» find a growing Dandelion plant (*Taraxacum officinale*) with a seed head (*but do not pick*)
» a gold spoon
» a white candle
» matches
» tongs
» a piece of paper
» a pen with gold ink

The Spell

Sit down next to the full Dandelion seed head and say:

Oh lovely seeds, ready to blow,

Will you grant my wishes everywhere that you go?

Dig a little hole in the soil with the gold spoon close to the Dandelion plant without disturbing the roots. Light your candle and say:

Seelie Faeries so busy and true,

I'll do your job if you help me too.

Write down your wish on the piece of paper with your gold-inked pen. Make sure you are as detailed as possible and say exactly what it is you desire and the time you would like it to occur.

Using the tongs, carefully burn the paper in the candle flame and say three times:

Alive in the fire, grow my desires.

Drop the ashes into the hole and cover with soil.

Thinking of your wish as clearly as possible, lean forward and blow the seeds from the Dandelion – you can pick it first of you like.

Thank the Seelie in whichever way you please – your own words are best – and place a lovely offering near the Dandelion plant.

To change the luck, fortune or energy of those in your home for the better, bury a Dandelion seed head in the north-east corner of your garden or perimeter and it should bring a favourable 'change in the wind'.

To send a secret message to someone special, think of it and blow a Dandelion seed head in their direction.

Jasmine Faerie Hope Body Wash Spell

The Jasmine Faerie is well known for helping people focus on increasing their resources as well as instilling hope and lifting moods. This lovely body wash will not only help you wash away your worries and negative feelings but help you gain a brighter outlook. This will make you much more likely to attract the positive things you want in life.

Timings
Full Moon, Saturday, Midday

Find and Gather
» 1 orange
» 2 tablespoons of dried Jasmine flowers (*Jasminum officinale*)
» 1 tablespoon of Orange Blossom flowers (*optional*) (*Citrus × sinensis*)
» 8 drops of Jasmine essential oil
» 4 drops of orange essential oil
» 2 tablespoons of coconut oil
» ½ cup of distilled water or rainwater
» ½ cup of grated goats milk soap
» 2 tablespoons of glycerin

- » a double boiler or alternative
- » a heat-proof mixing bowl
- » a funnel
- » a sterilised bottle with lid

The Spell

Peel the orange and add the peel to the mixing bowl with the flowers, then say:

Flowers of abundance, of hope and victory,

Dance with sweet orange and bring something nice to me.

Faerie of Jasmine,

I'm grateful for all you do for me.

Boil the water, pour over and cover. Leave for an hour, then strain and return to the bowl. Melt the coconut oil in the double boiler over a low heat. Transfer to your mixing bowl and stir in the glycerin, grated goats milk soap and essential oils.

Pour into the bottle using the funnel, saying:

Wash me with hope,

A brighter future I'll see,

Bring light and abundance,

Happiness and glee.

You can keep this magickal body wash in the fridge for two months. Use it in a bath or shower on a body buffer or on its own. Repeat the last chant each time you use it to empower you with hope and lift your attitude and mood.

To solve a problem, eat an orange and as you do, think long and hard about your challenge. Retain all the pips you come across. Once finished, an odd number of pips mean 'Yes' or a positive outcome; an even number means 'No' or a negative outcome.

Wearing Jasmine is a way to attract money and opportunities to make money. This flower is also strongly associated with love and good luck, and smelling its perfume can lead to dreams of a prophetic nature.

The Tündér Faerie Good Fortune Spell

The word 'Tündér' is the Hungarian word for Faerie. There, they are thought to be beautiful, friendly, human-like beings who live in castles in the high mountains and possess great wealth. Take time to draw a line in the earth and change your luck with this magickal tea. Raspberry leaf will bring you Faerie blessings and will help to improve your health or love prospects as well. Dandelion root is also aligned with Faerie energies and will bring you good luck. Orange peel is another luck-drawing addition to your magickal tea.

Timings
Waxing, Monday, Morning

Find and Gather
» a beautiful teapot
» a gorgeous teacup and saucer
» 1 teaspoon of Raspberry leaf (*Rubus idaeus*) tea
» 1 teaspoon of Dandelion root (*Taraxacum officinale)*
» 1 slice of orange peel
» boiling water
» a string of pearls or a single pearl
» a stick

The Spell

Find a lovely place outside to create your tea, but you can also make this tea at home, put it into a thermos and go to a lovely place in Nature to create a change in your fortune.

Place your Raspberry leaf tea in the pot and say:

Faerie blessings,

From berries so bright.

Add the Dandelion root and say:

The luck of the good.

Toss in the orange peel and say:

Sweet change of fortune,

Come to me.

Pour in the boiling water and say:

Tumble and mix,

Steep and just be.

The winds of good fortune,

Come to me.

Take the stick and draw a line in the earth, step over it and put on your pearls (or hold a single one in your hand), then sit and drink your tea.

These Faeries have a curious gift: their body fluids create precious jewels and metals. Their tears become pearls that they generously gift to the poor.

The Tündér are also shapeshifters and as well as being able to become invisible, can turn into animals, birds, fish and trees.

Will-ó-the-Wisps Traveller's Spell

I've always thought of Will-ó-the-Wisps as any sort of negative influence or energy that will take people off-track adversely or cause harm when travelling and so this spell is a traveller's protection spell. The inclusion of singing quartz crystals will keep you in the here and now and stop you becoming entranced and taken away. Lovage offers general safety and also protection from disease; both handy for travellers.

Timings

Full Moon, Saturday, Night

Find and Gather

Ignis Fatuus.

» 3 small singing quartz crystals (*they must be able to fit into the bottle*)
» a small sterilised glass spray bottle
» 1 small Lovage flower or leaf (*Levisticum officinale*)
» a few drops of glycerin
» spring water
» a small funnel (*optional*)

The Spell

You need to create this spell in a place that you feel completely safe, grounded and happy (preferably your home). This is because you are capturing the imprint of a place that you will return to.

Place the singing crystals into the bottle and place on the ground.

Walk around the bottle and say:

No matter where I wander,

No matter where I roam,

If something takes away,

My will to never be,

The crystals here will sing,

And bring me back to thee.

Fill the bottle with the spring water (using the funnel if need be). Add the Lovage and the glycerin (this is added to keep your mixture fresh).

To use: while travelling, each morning before you set off on your adventures, spray a little in the air before you and walk through it.

Will-ó-the-Wisps are found in the folklore of many cultures around the world. They usually appear to humans as sparkling lights under the surface of water or as hovering balls of light and are also known to create frightening sounds. They draw people in and they become entranced and may then be drowned or carried away by the Will-ó-the-Wisp.

The Latin for this Faerie being is *Ignis fatuus* which translates as 'foolish fire'. In Gaelic, it's *Teine biorach*, which means 'sharp fire'.

Parsley Faerie Winning Words Spell

If you are going to present, pitch or even attend a job interview, this spell will help you communicate in a winning way. The Parsley Faerie offers protection and the ability to win, and opens pathways to useful knowledge, so the inclusion of this herb will be helpful in any of these situations. Mint will help attract abundance and success to you as well. You can store this magickal mixture in the fridge for up to two weeks.

Timings

Waxing Moon, Wednesday, Evenings

Find and Gather

» 1 tablespoon of dried Parsley (*Petroselinum crispum*)

» 1 tablespoon of dried Mint (*Mentha* spp.)

» 1 cup of boiling water

» a heat-proof glass bowl

» a sieve

» a sterilised clear glass jar and lid

» 1 tablespoon of apple cider vinegar

» a tiny pinch of salt

The Spell

Place the Parsley and Mint in the glass bowl. Pour boiling water over to cover and say:

Parsley and mint,
Share your whispers and hints,
The words that I speak,
Be clear and at peak.

Leave for an hour, then strain into the glass jar. Add the apple cider vinegar and pinch of salt, and say:

Cider to clear,
Salt to ground.

To use: every evening for three days before you are to speak or be interviewed. Shake the jar well and use a few tablespoons to rinse your mouth for a few minutes. Do not swallow.

After spitting out, say:

Words that will follow,
Be strong, clear and right.
That which I say,
Win through from this night.

Mint is a good addition to spells to increase finances and inspire abundance. Its warming energy will bring success to plans that involve growth and inspiration.

Parsley is one of the very best magickal herbs to add to a bath if you need purification and energetic cleansing. The Ancient Greeks would wear Parsley at feasts as they believed it made them more attractive.

SECTION THREE

How to Create Your Own Faerie Spells

Ḟow to Create Your Own Ḟaerie Spells

❧ USING PLANTS IN SPELLS

To use a plant or flower in a spell you should understand its energy and to do this, you need to know its meaning and attributes. You can discover these by exploring the properties it has or look to aromatherapy, herbal medicine guides and botanical history resources.

❧ MAGICKAL CORRESPONDENCES

You may wish to create a bath, an essence, a tea, a mandala – in fact, anything at all which will be in itself an action related to the energy of the spell. Items required for this should be aligned with your outcome. These are usually called *Correspondences* or *Magickal Correspondences*. To expand your knowledge in areas that you do not have experience with, seek out resources that specialise in the item you wish to include, such as Astrological, Crystal, Colour and so on. Following is a beginning list of such correspondences to get you started:

Colour

You can use colour in cloths to set your spell upon, in the tools that you use, candles, in the flowers themselves and in additional ingredients.

Red: passion, power, strength, courage, renewal, health, motivation, self-esteem, confrontation, ambition, challenge, purchases

Pink: healing, calming, emotions, harmony, compassion, self-love, romance, relaxation, new beginnings, partnerships

Orange: opportunities, legal matters, obstacles, abundance, gain, power, happiness

Yellow: friendship, returns, productivity, creativity, education, healing

Green: wellness, new beginnings, marriage, home, planning, peace, harmony, birth, rebirth, fertility, affection, luck, change, creativity, socialising

Blue: self-improvement, opportunity, charity, study, growth, travel, insight, patience, meditation, sports, religion, social standing, expansion, higher education, wisdom

Brown: focus, lost items, grounding, harvest, security, generosity, endurance

Violet: psychic growth, divination, spiritual development, self-improvement

Purple: spirit, ambition, protection, healing, intuition, business, occultism

White: protection, safety, transformation, enlightenment, connection to higher self, becoming more outgoing, relieving shyness, the cycle of life, freedom, health, initiation

Black: divination, rebirth, material gain, discoveries, truth, sacrifice, protection, creation, death, karma, absorbing energies, binding, neutralising, debts, separation

Timings

These are the times that you put spells together and when they are cast. They add an energetic boost to your spells by bringing alignment to what you are doing in the space you are creating it. I'm sharing simple ones here for you but you can also explore deeper seasonal timings, ones associated with traditional pagan celebrations and observances and ones that are unique to the area and people where you live and are open to others.

MOON PHASES

Waxing: new projects, beginnings, growth

Full: empowerment, healing, attainment

Waning: banishing, cleansing, letting go

New: divination, revelations

DAY OF THE WEEK

Monday: home, family, dreams, emotions, female energies, gardens, medicine, psychic development, travel

Tuesday: courage, strength, politics, conflict, lust, endurance, competition, surgical procedures, sports, masculine energies

Wednesday: communication, divination, self-improvement, teaching, inspiration, study, learning

Thursday: luck, finances, legal matters, desires, honour, accomplishments, prosperity, material gain

Friday: friendship, pleasure, art, music, social activities, comfort, sensuality, romance

Saturday: life, protection, self-discipline, freedom, wisdom, goals, re-incarnation

Sunday: spirituality, power, healing, individuality, hope, healing, professional success, business

TIME OF THE DAY

Dawn: beginnings, awakening, cleansing, new ideas, change, love

Morning: growth, home, gardening, finances, harmony, generosity

Midday: health, willpower, physical energy, intellect

Afternoon: communication, business, clarity

Dusk/Twilight: reduction, change, receptiveness

Night: pleasure, joy, socialising, gatherings, play

Midnight: endings, release, recuperation

Crystals

The addition of crystals in the form of whole pieces, tumble stones, balls and jewellery can add the energies of each to your spell. Not all crystals are suitable for all types of spells as some are not safe when coming in contact with items you use for consumption, or topically.

Check these with a reliable specialised crystal usage resource as you create your spells.

Agate: courage, longevity, love, protection, healing, self-confidence

Agate, Black: success, courage

Agate, Black and White: physical protection

Agate, Blue Lace: peace, consciousness, peace, trust, self-expression

Agate, Green Moss: healing, longevity, gardening, harmony, abundance

Amazonite: creativity, unity, success, thought process

Amber: protection, luck, health, calming, humour, spell-breaker, manifestation

Amethyst: peace, love, protection, courage, happiness, psychic protection

Apache Tear: protection from negative energy, grief, danger, forgiveness

Apatite: control, communication, coordination

Aquamarine: calm, strength, control, fears, tension relief, thought processes

Aventurine: independence, money, career, sight, intellect, sport, leadership

Azurite: divination, healing, illusions, communication, psychic development

Bloodstone: healing, business, strength, power, legal matters, obstacles

Calcite: purification, money, energy, spirituality, happiness

Carnelian: courage, sexual energy, fear, sorrow release, action, motivation

Chalcedony: emotions, honesty, optimism

Chrysocolla: creativity, female energies, communication, wisdom

Citrine: detox, abundance, regeneration, cleansing, clarity, initiative

Dioptase: love attracter, prosperity, health, relaxation

Emerald: wealth, protection, intellect, artistic talent, tranquility, memory

Epidote: emotional healing, spirituality

Fluorite: study, intellect, comprehension, balance, concentration

Garnet: protection, strength, movement, confidence, devotion

Gold: power, success, healing, purification, honour, masculine energy

Hematite: divination, common sense, grounding, reasoning, relationships

Herkimer Diamond: tension-soothing, sleep, rest, power booster

Iolite: soul connection, visions, discord release

Jade: justice, wisdom, courage, modesty, charity, dreams, harmony

Jasper: healing, health, beauty, nurturing, travel

Jet: finances, nightmare protection, divination, health, luck, calms fears

Kunzite: addiction, maturity, security, divinity

Kyanite: dreams, creativity, vocalisation, clarity, serenity, channelling

Labradorite: destiny, elements

Lapis Lazuli: love, fidelity, joy, healing, psychic development, inner truth

Larimar: confidence, depression, serenity, energy balance

Malachite: money, sleep, travel, protection, business

Moldavite: changes, transformation, life purpose

Moonstone: youth, habits, divination, love, protection, friends

Obsidian: grounding, production, peace, divination

Onyx: stress, grief, marriage, nightmare protection, self-control

Opal: beauty, luck, power, money, astral projection

Pearl: faith, integrity, innocence, sincerity, luck, money, love

Peridot: wealth, stress, fear, guilt, personal growth, health

Prehnite: chakras, relationships

Pyrite: memory, focus, divination, luck

Quartz, Clear: protection, healing, power, psychic power

Quartz, Rose: love, peace, happiness, companionship

Quartz, Smoky: depression, negativity, tension, purification

Rhodochrosite: new love, peace, energy, mental powers, trauma healing

Ruby: wealth, mental balance, joy, power, contentment, intuition

Sapphire: meditation, protection, power, love, money, wisdom, hope

Sardonyx: progression, finances, self-protection

Selenite: decisions, reconciliation, flexibility, clarity

Silver: stress, travel, invocation, dreams, peace, protection, energy

Sodalite: wisdom, prophetic dreams, dissipates confusion

Sugilite: physical healing, heart, wisdom, spirituality

Sunstone: sexual healing, energy, protection, health

Tanzanite: magick, insight, awareness

Tiger's Eye: courage, money, protection, divination, energy, luck

Topaz: love, money, sleep, prosperity, commitment, calm

Tourmaline: friendship, business, health, astral projection

Tourmaline, Black: grounding, protection,

Tourmaline, Blue: peace, stress relief, clear speech

Tourmaline, Green: success, creativity, goals, connection with Nature

Tourmaline, Pink: friendship, love, creativity

Tourmaline, Red: projection, courage, energy

Turquoise: protection, communication, socialising, health, creative solutions

❦ FLOWER MEANINGS

Of course many plants have flowers and you can use books or resources that explore their meanings and uses to develop your own spells. Flowers hold the same energy as the rest of the plant. In fact, they offer an additional boost to the plant's energy because the plant is in the process of reproduction.

Here are some of the plants used in the spells in this book, and others you may find useful for your own spells. You can find a comprehensive list in my book *Flowerpaedia, 1000 Flowers and their Meanings* (Rockpool Publishing, Sydney, Australia, 2017)

Agrimony (*Agrimonia eupatoria*)*:* do not worry, inner fears and worries

Allspice (*Pimenta dioica*)*:* you are worthy, self value, self nurture

Angelica (*Angelica archangelica*): inspiration, spiritual protection, facing the unknown, protection

Basil (*Ocimum basilicum*): travel well, open heart, compassion, strengthen faith, spirituality, peace, love, fidelity, virtue, preservation, mourning, courage in difficulties, harmony

Burdock (*Arctium* spp.): do not touch me, protection, healing, persistence, importunity, core issues, release anger

Cardamom (*Elettario caramomum*)*:* love, lust

Catnip (*Nepeta cataria*): calm hysteria, clarity, focus, female healing

Chamomile, German (*Matricaria chamomilla*): equilibrium, relax, calm down, release tension, soothing, ease nightmares, energy, patience in adversity, nervous system support, love, attract love

Chamomile, Roman: (*Chamaemelum nobile*): I admire your courage, do not despair, love in austerity, patience, abundance, attract wealth, fortitude, calm

Chicory (*Cichorium intybus*): I love you unconditionally, removal of obstacles, invisibility, momentum, release of tension, favours, frigidity, unconditional love

Chives (*Allium schoenoprasum*): protection from evil spirits, protection of house, weight-loss, protection, long life

Cinnamon (*Cinnamomum verum*): forgiveness of hurt, clairvoyance, creativity, defence, divination, dreams, healing, love, mediation, psychic development, purification, spirituality, success, wealth, power

Clover (*Trifolium* spp.): good luck, fertility, domestic virtue, fortune, second sight

Clover, Red (*Trifolium pretense*): good fortune, good luck, fertility, domestic virtue, protection from danger, psychic protection, cleansing, clear negativity, balance, calmness, clarity, enhance self-awareness

Cloves (*Eugenia caryophyllata*): protection, dignity, exorcism, love, money

Coltsfoot (*Tussilago farfara*): I am concerned for you, maternal love, concern, children, new challenges, vitality, physical stamina, immunity

Comfrey (*Symphytum officinale*): healing, fusion

Dandelion (*Taraxacum officinale*): I am faithful to you, your wish is granted, long lasting happiness, healing, intelligence, warmth, power, clarity, survival

Dill (*Anethum graveolens*): lust, luck, protection from evil, finances

Echinacea (*Echinacea purpurea*): higher self, strength, physical strength, immunity, healing, dignity, wholeness, integrity

Foxglove (*Digitalis purpurea*): I believe in you, beware, stateliness, communication, insincerity, magick, confidence, creativity, youth

Frankincense (*Boswellia sacra*): faithful heart, blessing, consecration, courage, divination, energy, exorcism, love, luck, meditation, power, protection, purification, spiritual growth, spirituality, strength, success, visions

Gardenia (*Gardenia jasminoides*): awareness, secret love, divine message

Garlic (*Allium sativum*): good fortune, protection, strength, courage, aphrodisiac, wholeness, immunity

Ginger (*Zingiber officinale*): you are loved, clarity, determination, intelligence, courage, warm feelings, tension relief, sensitivity, perception, sensory awareness

Ginkgo (*Gingko biloba*): beauty, business, calling spirits, dreams, fertility, longevity, love

Ginseng (*Panax* spp.): love, wishes, beauty, protection, lust, grounding, balance, disconnection, longevity, mental powers

Goldenseal (*Hydrastis canadensis*): healing, money

Gotu Kola (*Hydrocotyle asiatica*): self-awareness

Guarana (*Paullinia cupana*): wishes, energy

Hawthorn (*Crataegus monogyna*): balance, duality, purification, sacred union, hope, heart protection

Honeysuckle (*Lonicera* spp.): Be happy, I am devoted to you, happiness, sweet disposition, sweet life, end arguments, homesickness, intimacy, unity

Hop (*Humulus lupulus*): apathy, injustice, passion, pride, healing, sleep, mirth

Hyssop (*Hyssopus officinalis*): I forgive you, cleanliness, sacrifice, breath, forgiveness, purification, shame, guilt, pardon, repentance

Juniper (*Juniperus communis*): journey, protection, anti-theft, love, exorcism, health, healing, cleansing, purifying spaces

Laurel (*Laurus nobilis*): I change but in death, I admire you but cannot love you, victory, protection from disease, protection from witchcraft, merit, glory

Lavender (*Lavandula* spp.): cleansing, protection, grace, trust, I admire you

Lemon Balm (*Melissa officinalis*): lift spirits, renewed youth, calm, strengthen mind, restore health, vigour, balance emotions, relax, courage, inner strength

Lemon Verbena (*Aloysia triphylla*): attractiveness, love, protection from nightmares, sweet dreams, marriage, purification

Lemongrass (*Cymbopogon citratus*): friendship, lust, psychic awareness, purification, protection from snakes

Marshmallow (*Althea officinalis*): to cure, humanity, dispel evil spirits, attract good spirits, beneficence, mother, maternal energies, protection

Meadowsweet (*Filipendula ulmaria*): healing, love, divination, peace, happiness, protection from evil, balance, harmony

Motherwort (*Leonurus cardiaca*): concealed love, female healing, inner trust, spiritual healing, astral travel, immortality, longevity, relationship balance, mothering issues, sedation, calm anxiety

Mugwort (*Artemisia vulgaris*): prophecy, protection, strength, psychic abilities, prophetic dreams, healing, astral projection, awkwardness, creative visualisation, visions, clairvoyance, divination

Nettle (*Urtica* spp.): you are cruel, you are spiteful, cruelty, pain, slander, clear choices, decision-making, protection against evil spirits, health recovery

Onion (*Allium cepa*): protection, purification, detox, hibernation, potential

Oregano (*Origanum vulgare*): joy, happiness, honour

Parsley (*Petroselinum crispum*): entertainment, feast, protection of food, festivity, to win, useful knowledge

Passionflower (*Passiflora incarnate*): I am pledged to another, belief, passion, religious superstition, religious work, stability, spiritual balance, higher consciousness

Patchouli (*Pogostemon cablin*): defence, fertility, releasing, love, wealth, sexual power

Peppermint (*Mentha piperita*): friendship, love, clarity, refreshment, concentration, clear thinking, inspiration, energy, alert mind, study support

Primrose (Primula vulgaris): patience, kindness, gentleness, belonging, courage

Primrose, Scottish (*Primula scotica*): I love you completely, I'm sorry, compassion, acceptance, anxiety, forgiveness, unconditional love, patience

Raspberry leaf (*Rubus idaeus*): compassion, generosity, envy, remorse

Rose (*Rosa* spp.)

» orange: fascination, enthusiasm, happiness

» peach: appreciation, agreement, sincerity

» pink: love, friendship

» red: courage, passion, respect, beauty

» white: truth, protection, honesty

» yellow: friendship, new beginning, second chances, welcome

Rosemary (*Rosmarinus officinalis*): I remember you, your presence revives me, psychic awareness, mental strength, accuracy, clarity, remembrance, memory

Sage (*Salvia officinalis*): purification, longevity, good health, long life, wisdom, cleansing, protection, higher purpose, reflection, inner peace, esteem, domestic virtue

Sandalwood (*Santalum album*): clear negativity, mental focus, reincarnation, wishes

Skullcap (*Scutellaria* spp.): relaxation, psychic healing, relaxation of nerves, self-esteem, ability to cope

Slippery Elm (*Ulmus rubra*): stop gossip

Sweet Marjoram (*Origanum marjorana*): let go of fear, self-reliance, comforting, relieve physical tension, relieve mental tension, consolation, protection from lightning, comfort grief, fertility, love, joy, honour, good fortune, long life

Thyme (*Thymus vulgaris*): bravery, affection, courage, strength, let's do something, activity

Valerian (Polemonium caeruleum): accommodating disposition, concealed merit

Wormwood (*Artemisia absinthium*): do not be discouraged, absence, authenticity, sorrowful parting

Yarrow (*Achillea millefolium*): friendship, war, elegance, banishing, relaxation

Flowerpaedia can also be used to look up energies and themes and so find flowers, herbs and plants that you wish to include in your spell. Here is a sample that you might find useful:

Change: Bee Balm (*Monarda* spp.), Scarlet Pimpernel (*Anagalis arvensis*), Mayflower (*Epigaea repens*), Fireweed (*Chamerion angustifolium*), Snowplant (*Sarcodes sanquinea*)

Clarity: Boronia (*Boronia ledifolia*), Grass Tree (*Xanthorrhoea resinosa*), Sweet Alyssum (*Alyssum maritimum*), Hemp (*Cannabis Sativa*), Angel's Trumpet (*Brugmansia candida*), Dandelion (*Taraxacum officinale*), Petunia (*Petunia* spp.), Hippeastrum (*Hippeastrum* spp.), Rosemary (*Rosmarinus officinalis*), Trout Lily (*Erythronium americanum*), Greater Celandine (*Chelidonium majus*), Peppermint (*Mentha piperita*), Catnip (*Nepeta cataria*), Clary Sage (*Salvia sclarea*), Red Clover (*Trifolium pretense*), Ginger (*Zingiber officinale*), Carrot (*Daucus carota* subsp. *sativus*), Grapefruit (*Citrus parasisi*), Coffee (*Coffea arabica*)

Clarity, emotional: Love-in-a-Mist (*Nigella damascene*), Gerbera Daisy (yellow) (*Gerbera jamesonii*)

Deceit: Mock Orange (*Philadelphus* spp.), Venus Flytrap (*Dionaea muscipula*), Lewis Mock Orange (*Philadelphus lewisii*), Dogbane (*Apocynum cannabinum*), Fly Orchid (*Ophrys insectifera*), Rocket (*Eruca sativa*)

Encouragement: Madonna Lily (*Lilium candidum*), Carnation, pink (*Dianthus caryophyllus*), Dahlia (*Dahlia* spp.), Goldenrod (*Solidago virgaurea*), Black-Eyed

Susan (*Rudbeckia hirta*), Campion, red (*Silene* spp.), Bayberry (*Myrica* spp.), Watermelon (*Citrullus lanatus*), Butterfly Lily (*Hedychium coronarium*)

Release: Lechenaultia (*Lechenaultia formas*), Henbane (*Hyoscyamus niger*), Calendula (*Calendula officinalis*), Skunk Cabbage (*Symplocarpus foetidus*), Alder (*Alnus*), Rose, meadow (*Rosa blanda*), Butterfly Weed (*Asclepias tuberosa*), Moneywort (*Bacopa monnieri*), Melilot (*Melilotus officinalis*), Air Plant (*Tillandsia* spp.)

Release anger: Burdock (*Arctium* spp.), Firethorn (*Pyracantha* spp.)

Release attachments: Trumpet Creeper (*Campisis radicans*)

Release barriers: Lady's Mantle (*Alchemilla vulgaris*)

Survival: Waratah (*Telopea speciosissima*), Dandelion (*Taraxacum officinale*), Tropicbird Orchid (*Angraecum eburneum*), Texas Bluebonnet (*Lupinus texensis*), Kapok (*Bomliax ceilia*)

YOUR FAERIE
SPELL JOURNAL

Title

....

Description

....

....

....

Find and Gather

....

....

....

The Spell

....

....

....

....

....

....

....

....

Title

....

Description

....

....

....

Find and Gather

....

....

....

The Spell

....

....

....

....

....

....

....

....

Title

....

Description

....

....

....

Find and Gather

....

....

....

The Spell

....

....

....

....

....

....

....

....

Title

....

Description

....

....

....

Find and Gather

....

....

....

The Spell

....

....

....

....

....

....

....

....

Title

....

Description

....

....

....

Find and Gather

....

....

....

The Spell

....

....

....

....

....

....

....

....

Title

....

Description

....

....

....

Find and Gather

....

....

....

The Spell

....

....

....

....

....

....

....

....

....

Ignis Fatuus.

Glossary of Magickal and Botanical Terms

apothecary: a storehouse or shop containing magickal supplies

basal: arising from the root crown of a plant

bract: a modified leaf which sometimes looks like a petal

bracteole: leaf-like projections

bulb: underground stem with modified leaves that contain stored food for plant shoot within

cardinal points: directions on a compass

cast: to create and release magick

compound leaf: a leaf with a division of two or more small leaf-like structures

corm: the underground bulb-like part of some plants

corona: a ring of structures which rise like a tube from a flower

cultivar: a plant that has agricultural or horticultural use and whose unique characteristics are reproduced during propagation

cut flower: a flower used as decoration

dominant hand: the hand you are more proficient with

endemic: native or restricted to a certain place

floret: one of the small flowers making up a flower head

flower head: a compact mass of flowers forming what appears to be a single flower

Full Moon: when the moon is fully visible as a round disk

genus: a group of organisms that are closely related in characteristics

grounded: to be fully connected with your physical being and the Earth

grounding: to bring yourself back into the everyday world

hermaphrodic (adj.): having both male and female reproductive parts

hermaphrodite (n): having both male and female reproductive parts

hex: a spell cast to cause harm

inflorescence: several flowers closely grouped together to form one unit or the particular arrangement of flowers on a plant

lanceolate: shaped like a lance, tapering to a point at each end

leaflet: a small leaf or leaf-like part or part of a compound leaf

leguminous: an erect or climbing bean or pea plant

lobe: a rounded or projected part

magick: metaphysical work to bring about change

mojo bag: a magic bag into which magickal items are placed and usually worn on the person

New Moon: the moon phase when the moon is not visible

oracle: a person who translates divination messages between the Other Worlds and people

ovate: egg-shaped with a broader end at the base

Pagan: originally meaning people who lived in the countryside and now meaning those who follow Nature-based spirituality and hold beliefs other than the main religions of the world

parasitic: gains all or part of its nutritional needs from another living plant

perennial: a plant which lives for three or more years

pericarpel: the cup-like structure of a flower on which the sepals, petals and stamens sit

pinnate: feather-like

pseudanthium: a flower head consisting of many tiny flowers

raceme: inflorescence in which the main axis produces a series of flowers on lateral stalks

ray flower: a flower which resembles a petal

ritual: a ceremony that features actions and sometimes words or music

scrying: using a reflective surface or a body of water in divination to gaze into

sessile: attached without a stalk

species (spp.): a group of organisms with a genus that are closely related and are usually about to interbreed.

spent: flowers or plants that are dead

stamen: the pollen producing reproductive organ of a flower

staminal column: a structure, in column form containing the male reproductive organ of plant

steep: to leave in hot water so that properties are imparted via heat into the water

stem: the main part of a plant, usually rising above the ground

tepal: a segment in a flower that has no differentiation between petals and sepals

thermogenic: the ability to generate own heat and maintain it

tuber: a thicken part of an underground stem

Waning Moon: the moon is getting smaller, towards dark/new

Waxing Moon: the moon is getting larger, towards full

Bibliography

Blier, Suzanne Preston, *African Vodun, Art, Psychology and Power* (University of Chicago Press 1995)

Cavendish, Lucy and Conneeley, Serene, *The Book of Faerie Magick* (Blessed Bee Publishing, 2010)

Cook, Will, *Indoor Gardening* (TCK Publishing 2013)

Coombes, Allen J. *Dictionary of Plant Names* (Timber Press 2002)

Cunningham, Scott, *Encyclopedia of Magical Herbs* (Llewellyn Publications 2010)

Graves, Julia, *The Language of Plants* (Lindisfarne Books 2012)

Hall, Dorothy, *The Book of Herbs* (Angus and Robertson 1972)

Hanson, J. Wesley, *Flora's Dial* (Jonathan Allen 1846)

Harrison, Lorraine, *RHS Latin for Gardeners* (Mitchell Beazley 2012)

Hemphill, John and Rosemary, *Myths and Legends of the Garden* (Hodder & Stoughton 1997)

Hill, Lewis and Hill, Nancy, *The Flower Gardener's Bible* (Storey Publishing 2003)

Kelly, Frances, *The Illustrated Language of Flowers* (Viking O'Neil 1992)

Macoboy, Stirling, *What Flower Is That?* (Lansdowne Press 2000)

Olds, Margaret, *Flora's Plant Names* (Gordon Cheers 2003)

Pavord, Anna, *The Naming of Names, The Search for Order in the World of Plants* (Bloomsbury 2005)

Phillips, Stuart, *An Encyclopaedia of Plants in Myth, Legend, Magic and Lore* (Robert Hale Limited 2012)

Telesco, Patricia, *A Floral Grimoire* (Citadel Press 2001)

Thomsen, Michael and Gennat, Hanni, *Phyotherapy Desk Reference* (Global Natural Medicine 2009)

Vickery, Roy, *A Dictionary of Plant-Lore* (Oxford University Press 1995)

Image Credits

Welcome

Hall, Mrs S. C., *Midsummer Eve: a Fairy Tale of Love* (J. C. Hotten, London, 1870)

How to Use This Book

Jenkins, William Henry Jeffrey, *How Tom Jeffrey Saw the World* (Simpkin, Marshall. & Co, London, 1897)

What Is a Spell and How Does It Work?

Hall, Mrs S. C., *Midsummer Eve: a Fairy Tale of Love* (J. C. Hotten, London, 1870)

How to Create and Cast a Spell

Smith, Henry John, ill: Niemeyer, A., *Dramatic Works and Minor Poems* (W. Ridgway, London, 1891)

Connecting with Faeries for Magickal Work

Shakespeare, William, Ill: Raymond, Robert Reikes, *Typical Tales of Fancy, Romance, and History from Shakespeare's Plays* (Fords, Howard, and Hulbert, New York, 1892)

Ingredients and Tools for Spells

Bradley, Gertrude M. and Mark, Amy, *New Pictures in Old Frames* (Simpkin & Marshall, London, 1894)

A Collection of Faerie Spells

Shakespeare, William, Ill: Raymond, Robert Reikes, *Typical Tales of Fancy, Romance, and History from Shakespeare's Plays* (Fords, Howard, and Hulbert, New York, 1892)

Faerie Garden and Nature Spells

Grandville, J. J., *Les fleurs animées* vol. 1 (1867)

Celandine Faerie Guide Flower Spell

Quiller-Couch, Sir Arthur. Ill: Dulac, Edmund, *The Sleeping Beauty and Other Fairy Tales* (Hodder & Stoughton, London, England 1910)

Curupira Animal Protection Spell

Lang, Andrew. Ill: Ford, H. J. and Speed, Lancelot, *The Blue Poetry Book* (Longmans & Co., London, 1891)

Foxglove Faerie Magick Garden Spell

Andersen, Hans Christian, Ill: Tegner, Hans, *Fairy Tales and Stories* (New York: The Century Co, 1900).

Faerie Nature Glitter Boundary Spell

Du Chaillu, Paul Belloni., *Stories of the Gorilla Country, etc,* (London, 1868)

Meadowsweet Faerie Pendulum Spell

Beard, Lina and Beard, Adelia B., *Things Worth Doing and How to Do Them* (Scribner's, New York, 1906)

Tylwyth Teg Faeries Bumper Harvest Spell

Shakespeare, William. Ill: Robinson, W. Heath, *Shakespeare's Comedy of a Midsummer Night's Dream* (H. Holt, New York, 1914)

Dryad Nature Protection Spell

Dodge, Mary Mapes, *St. Nicholas* [serial], (Scribner & Co., New York 1873)

Thyme Faerie See the Fae Spell

Planché, James Robinson, *An Old Fairy Tale* (London, 1865)

Deva Faerie Connection Spell

Twain, Mark (Clemens, Samuel L). Ill: Brown, Walter Francis, *A Tramp Abroad* (Chatto & Windus, London 1880)

Trädandar Faerie Wishes Tree Spell

Charpentier's Illustrated Guide to Southsea, the Dockyard, Isle of Wight, etc, (W. H. Charpentier & Co., Portsmouth, 1892)

Faerie Love and Friendship Spells

Sudds, W. F., *Fairy Revels* (Thompson & Odell, Boston, Mass, 1844)

Rose Faerie New Love Spell

von Holst, Theodor, *The Fairy Lovers* (circa 1840)

Faerie Heal a Broken Heart Spell

Herford, Oliver, *Artful Anticks* (Gray & Co., London, 1894)

Ambrosia Faerie Romantic Spark Grow Spell
  Hall, Mrs S. C., *Midsummer Eve: a Fairy Tale of Love* (J. C. Hotten, London, 1870

Crocus Time to Love Again Spell
  Gordon, Elizabeth, Ill: Volland, Joliet, *Flower Children* (Boston, 1910)

Iolanthe Clear Away Misunderstandings Spell
  Dalziel, D, ill: McVickar, H. W., *A Parody on Iolanthe* illustrated (1883)

Aine See the Light of Love Spell
  Hood, Thomas, Ill: Brock, Charles Edmund, *Humorous Poems* (Macmillan & Co. London, 1893)

Honeysuckle Faerie Send Happiness Spell
  Gardiner, Ruth Kimball and Kimball, Frances Palmer, *In Happy far-away Land* (Zimmerman's, New York, 1902)

Folletti Faerie Harmony and Happiness Spell
  Crane, Walter, *A Floral Fantasy in an Old English Garden* (Harper & Bros., London, 1899)

Violet and Pansy Loving Honey Spell
  Grandville, J. J., *Les fleurs animées* vol. 1 (1867)

Faerie Truffles Happy Gathering Spell
  Dodge, Mary Elizabeth, *When Life is Young,* (Century Co., New York, 1894)

Faerie Healing and Protection Spells
  Shakespeare, William, Raymond, Robert Reikes, *Typical Tales of Fancy, Romance and History from Shakespeare's Plays* (Fords, Howard, and Hulbert, New York, 1892)

Alven Faerie Water Energy Spell
  Lang, Andrew, *The Yellow Fairy Book* (Longmans, Green, And Co., London, New York, 1906)

Mallow Faerie True Voice Spell
  Hall, Mrs S. C., *Midsummer Eve: a Fairy Tale of Love* (London, 1848)

Morgan Le Fey Daily Health Spell
  Sandys, Frederick, *Morgan-le-Fay* (1863–64)

Nephelae Emotion Calming Spell
  Holland, Samuel, *The Victrola Book of the Opera* (Victor Talking Machine Co., Camden, N. J., 1917)

Rosemary Faerie Mental Clarity Spell

Hall, Mrs S. C., *Midsummer Eve: a Fairy Tale of Love* (London, 1848)

De Grossman Stop Bad Behaviour Spell

Ford, H. J., *The Violet Fairy Book* (Longmans, Green; London, New York, 1906)

The Vila Faerie Battle Spell

Smith, George Barnett., *Illustrated British Ballads, Old and New* (1894)

Hibiscus Faerie Purification Spell

Baker, Lucy D. Sale, *Illustrated Poems and Songs for Young People* (G. Routledge & Sons, London, 1885)

Trooping Faerie Change Luck Spell

Gale, Norman Rowland. Ill: Stratton, Helen, *Songs for Little People* (Constable & Co. London, 1896)

Queen Mab's Secret Keeper Spell

Shakespeare, William, Ill: Raymond, Robert Reikes, *Typical Tales of Fancy, Romance, and History from Shakespeare's Plays* (Fords, Howard, and Hulbert, New York, 1892)

Faerie Home and Family Spells

Lang, Andrew, Ill: Ford, Henry Justice, *The Olive Fairy Book* (Longmans, Green, London New York, 1907)

Lavender Faerie Sweep Away Spell

Nineteenth century French greeting card

Gårdstomte Pet Healing Spell

Hall, Mrs S. C., *Midsummer Eve: a Fairy Tale of Love* (London, 1848)

Bean Tighe Faerie Family Helper Spell

Baum, L. Frank, Ill: Neill, John R., *The Road to Oz* (Reilly & Lee, Chicago, 1909)

Faerie Chai Time Sleepy Tea Spell

Herford, Oliver. *Artful Anticks* (Gray & Co., London, 1894)

Faerie Dreams Banish Nightmares Spell

Shakespeare, William, Ill: Raymond, Robert Reikes, *Typical Tales of Fancy, Romance, and History from Shakespeare's Plays* (Fords, Howard, and Hulbert, New York, 1892)

Aziza Faerie Study Spell

Hall, Mrs S. C., *Midsummer Eve: a Fairy Tale of Love* (J. C. Hotten, London, 1870)

Oosood Faerie New Baby Spell

Hall, Mrs S. C., *Midsummer Eve: a Fairy Tale of Love* (J. C. Hotten, London, 1870)

Brownie Strawberry Flower Gratitude Spell
Cox, Palmer. *The Brownies at Home* (T. Fisher Unwin, London; New York, 1893)

Attract Faerie Friends Spell
Gale, Norman Rowland., Stratton, Helen, *Songs for Little People* (Constable & Co.: London, 1896)

Pixie Increase Circle of Friends Spell
Hall, Mrs S. C., *Midsummer Eve: a Fairy Tale of Love* (J. C. Hotten, London, 1870)

Faerie Beauty and Spa Spells
Lang, Andrew, Ill: Ford, H. J., *The Olive Fairy Book* (Longmans, Green, London, New York, 1907)

Chamomile Faerie Morning Dew Spell
Hall, S. C. Mrs, *Midsummer Eve: a Fairy Tale of Love* (J. C. Hotten, London 1870)

Faerie Queen Titania Summer Bronzer
Shakespeare, William, Ill: Fredericks, Alfred, *A Midsummer Night's Dream* (D. Appleton and company, New York, 1874)

Apple Faerie Sweet Words Lip Balm
Baltimore and Ohio Employees Magazine (Baltimore, Baltimore and Ohio Railroad Company, 1920)

The Sidhe Elixir of Youth Spell
Grimm, Jacob, Grimm, Wilhelm, Ill: Rackham, Arthur, *The Fairy Tales of the Brothers Grimm* (New York, Doubleday, New York, 1916)

Faerie Rejuvenating Milk Bath Spell
Bradley, Gertrude M. and Mark, Amy, *New Pictures in Old Frames* (Simpkin & Marshall, London, 1894)

Moss Maiden Face Mask Spell
Doyle, Richard; Planché, James Robinson, *An Old Fairy Tale, The Sleeping Beauty* (London, 1865)

Ijósálfar Fae Face Mist Spell
Anderson, Isabel, *The Great Sea Horse* (Brown and company, Boston, 1909)

Ginger Faerie Sugar Scrub Spell
Cummings, W.H. *Songs and Lyrics for Little Lips* (London, 1879)

Daisy Faerie Feet Foot Soak Spell

Bradley, Gertrude M. and Mark, Amy, *New Pictures in Old Frames* (Simpkin & Marshall, London, 1894)

Calendula Faerie Hair Repair Spell

Collodi, Carlo, Ill: Folkard, Charles, *Pinocchio: the Tale of a Puppet* (J. M. Dent New York: E .P. Dutton, London, 1911)

Faerie Happiness and Wish Spells

Gale, Norman Rowland. Ill: Stratton, Helen, *Songs for Little People* (Constable & Co., London, 1896)

Sage Faerie Remove Negativity Spell

Hall, Mrs S. C., *Midsummer Eve: a Fairy Tale of Love* (J. C. Hotten, London, 1870)

Leprechaun Good Luck in Business Spell

Croker, T. C., *Fairy Legends and Traditions of the South of Ireland* (J. Murry, London, 1834)

Faerie Art Divination Spell

Field, Eugene, Ill: Robinson, Charles, *Lullaby-Land: Songs of Childhood* (G. N. Morang & Company: Toronto, 1900)

Bergamot Faerie Stop Worry Linen Spray

Gale, Norman Rowland. Ill: Stratton, Helen, *Songs for Little People* (Constable & Co.: London, 1896)

Tuatha dé Danann Creativity Spell

Pen and Pencil Pictures from the Poets (Edinburgh, 1866)

Seelie Dandelion Wish Spell

Nineteenth century French greeting card

Jasmine Faerie Hope Body Wash Spell

Waite, Arthur Edward. *Belle and the Dragon* (J. Elliott & Co. London, 1894)

The Tündér Faerie Good Fortune Spell

Gray, Major William, *Travels in Western Africa in the Years 1819–21,* London, 1825

Will-ó-the-Wisps Traveller's Spell

Jennings, John Joseph, *Theatrical and Circus Life* (Chicago, Laird & Lee, 1893)

Parsley Faerie Winning Words Spell

Hall, Mrs S. C., *Midsummer Eve: a Fairy Tale of Love* (London, 1848)

About the Author

Cheralyn Darcey is a botanical explorer, florist, organic gardener, environmental artist and the author and illustrator of over a dozen botanical titles. Through her books, she shares with readers her passion for nature and researching plants and their relationships with us. Living on the Central Coast of NSW, Australia, Cheralyn has created and nurtures her own extensive flower, vegetable and interesting plant home garden that has been featured in national publications and her creative sanctuary.

For more information, visit www.cheralyndarcey.com

Instagram: cheralyn

Youtube: Florasphere

Facebook: cheralyn.darcey

Other books by Cheralyn ...

The Book of Flower Spells

Beautiful to behold and sacred throughout time, flowers hold powerful nature magick, entwined with the rhythms of the Earth.

The Book of Herb Spells

Herbs can heal, comfort and nourish us with ancient energies used throughout time to create magickal spells.

The Book of Tree Spells

Powerful nature magick is yours when you learn the mystical way of the trees and listen well to their wisdom.

Available from all good bookstores or online at
www.rockpoolpublishing.com.au